You Shall Have Good Success

by
Kurtis Ward

Economics of the Kingdom
Oklahoma City, Oklahoma

You Shall Have Good Success
ISBN 0-88144-195-3
Copyright © 1995 by Kurtis J. Ward
Economics of the Kingdom
P. O. Box 21405
Oklahoma City, OK 73156

Published by Kurtis J. Ward

ENDORSEMENT
by Jerry Savelle

Dear Kurtis,

I really enjoyed your book and I appreciate your confidence in this ministry. I believe you truly tapped the wisdom of God for laying a good foundation for Christians to understand the will of our Heavenly Father regarding prosperity and success.

Anyone who will take the time to read your book with an open mind and a receptive heart will hear the voice of the Holy Spirit and will receive a divine impartation from Him concerning how God wants to bless their lives, especially in the area of finances.

Thanks for obeying God. This book will bless many.

In Him,

Jerry Savelle

DEDICATION

This book is dedicated to the three women in my life: To my mother, Brenda, who prayed and led me into the kingdom of God; to my wife, Regina, whose patience, support, and encouragement have already made this book a success; and to my daughter, Taylor, for when she looks at me and smiles with those big brown eyes—I'm even more able to comprehend what is the breadth and length, the depth and height, of our Heavenly Father's love toward His own children.

FOREWORD

God's will is for you to experience prosperity and success. For some reason many Christians never let go of the antiquated ideas passed along from uninformed believers, confused ministers and society itself that God has intended for His children to be poor and humble. Humility is a quality each of us should possess, but poverty is totally contrary to the very nature of God.

Kurtis Ward has compiled strategic scriptures with timely insight to lay a new foundation in your thinking or to fortify your current understanding about God's thoughts on success. This is the hour for believers and particularly Christian businessmen to settle this issue in their hearts and to learn that the responsibility lies with them to accept and experience what God has promised.

You'll learn sound biblical principles about such issues as meditation, the power of words, faith and more. The greatest success book in life is the Bible. So many pay thousands of dollars for seminars to learn about success when God offers it to you and me freely. There is a price to pay, but not in the way the world may think.

Enjoy reading this revealing book. Let the contents saturate your mind and remove any doubts about God's commitment towards you. God is no respecter of persons. What He has done for Kurtis concerning success, He is ready to do for you.

Kirk Pankratz
Senior Pastor
Church of the Harvest
Oklahoma City, Oklahoma

INTRODUCTION

The purpose of this book is to expound on what God's Word says about success. Everyone has different ideas of what "true success" really is. Money, material possessions, fame, power...the list goes on and on. While the above items *can* be a measure of success, many of us know people who have achieved great amounts of money, material possessions, fame, and power, but their lives have been anything but a "success." This has caused some people to reach the erroneous conclusion that if you desire prosperity and success (or if you're already prosperous), you are not in line with God's Word.

Is this true? What does God's Word say about prosperity and success? Does His Word really make financial promises to us or is everyone supposed to take "a vow of poverty"? Why are there so many different viewpoints both in the world and the church regarding the prosperity message? What are the economic laws operating within the kingdom of God? Is there anything wrong with becoming a success? If not, how can one achieve success according to God's Word?

After reading the contents of this book, you may be quite surprised to learn how much of the Bible deals with money, power, possessions, inheritances, stewardship, building, buying, selling, ruling, prosperity and success. In fact, there are over 1,500 such verses in the Bible. Also, you will find several "TIPS" that will prove quite helpful in achieving greater success in life.

Almost every scripture is shown in its entirety so that it cannot be taken out of context. You will probably want to mark many of the scriptures contained within this book in your own Bible for later reference.

It is my desire to ignite a flame in your heart for the Word of God, which contains the answers for everything in life.

Kurtis Ward

CONTENTS

CHAPTER 1
YOU SHALL HAVE
GOOD SUCCESS

**This book of the law shall not depart out of thy
mouth; but thou shalt meditate therein day and night,
that thou mayest observe to do according to all that is
written therein: for then thou shalt make thy way
prosperous, and then *thou shalt have good success.***
Joshua 1:8

The title of this book, *You Shall Have Good Success*,
sounds as though it is a command from God. However, the
"secret to success " is to understand that success is a
condition in God's Word.

When we think of *success,* our minds are instantly
flooded with pictures of money, mansions, new cars, nice
clothes, high–paying jobs, etc. However, the definition of
success can mean different things to different people. A
person who has no money might think of himself as being
successful if he was to become a millionaire. However, a
billionaire would look at himself as *unsuccessful* if he was
reduced to a millionaire. This shows us that *success* can be
relative to individual interpretation, but what does the
Bible really say about being a success?

After looking up the word *success* in a *Strong's
Concordance,* we find that the *King James Version's* authors
translated the original Hebrew word as *success* only once in
the whole Bible. So that they be not accused of a
mistranslation, it would be prudent for us to review the
meaning of the original Hebrew word.

The Hebrew word for *success* in Joshua 1:8 is *sakal* pronounced "saw–kal" which is inclusive of the following meanings: *"to be circumspect and hence intelligent, consider, expert, instruct, prosper, deal prudently, give skillfully, have good success, teach, have and make to understand wisdom, behave wisely, and guide wittingly."* (*Strong's Concordance* 7919.)

This is God's definition of "good" success.

Joshua (Israel's new commander–in–chief) carefully chose this Hebrew word as he was speaking to the children of Israel just after the death of Moses. In three days they would be crossing the Jordan River to go in and possess the promised land. Let's look again at his words, this time paying attention to the second to the last phrase of this scripture.

> **This book of the law shall not depart out of thy mouth; but thou shalt meditate therein day and night, that thou mayest observe to do according to all that is written therein: for then *thou shalt make thy way prosperous*, and then thou shalt have good success.**
> **Joshua 1:8**

The word *prosperous* in this phrase comes from the Hebrew word *tsaleach* pronounced "tsaw–lay'–akh" which means, *"to push forward, break out, come mightily, go over, be good, be meet, be profitable, cause to prosper."* (*Strong's Concordance* 6743.)

It seems Joshua was preaching a "prosperity and success" sermon to the people just before they crossed over into the promised land. Their prosperity and success were conditioned upon three things: *speaking the Word, meditating the Word,* and *observing and doing the Word.*

TIP #1
Purchase a KJV *Strong's Exhaustive Concordance of the Bible.* Use it to discover original Hebrew (Old Testament) and Greek (New Testament) words and their meanings. This will help increase your knowledge of the meanings of key words found in Scripture.

According to God's Word, prosperity and success are not such bad things after all. God wants to bring success upon all His children. Did you know that He delights in the prosperity of those who serve Him?

> **Let them shout for joy, and be glad, that favour my righteous cause: yea, let them say continually, Let the Lord be magnified,** *which hath pleasure in the prosperity of his servant.*

> **Psalm 35:27**

But remember, this "prosperity and good success" is conditioned on three things:

1. Speaking the Word – "Shall not depart out of your mouth." (This may appear to be a contradiction, but "shall not depart" actually means "don't quit." The Word should be constantly coming out of your mouth.)

2. Meditating on the Word – "Shall meditate day and night."

3. Observe and Do the Word – "Observe and do according to."

This sounds very similar to the first Psalm:

> *Blessed is the man* **that walketh not in the counsel of the ungodly, nor standeth in the way of sinners, nor sitteth in the seat of the scornful.**

> **But his delight is in the law of the Lord; and in his law doth he meditate day and night.**

> **And he shall be like a tree planted by the rivers of water, that bringeth forth his fruit in his season; his leaf also shall not wither; and** *whatsoever he doeth shall prosper.*

> **Psalm 1:1-3**

In the 1970's and 80's, the power of positive thinking was a popular teaching. However, in the first Psalm, God's Word starts out in the negative.

11

The man who prospers will *not*:

1. *Walk* in the counsel of the ungoldy.

2. *Stand* in the way of sinners.

3. *Sit* in the seat of the scornful.

Who are the ungodly? The morally wrong, the wicked, the unjust.

Who are the sinners? Those who miss the mark and pass the limits of the law.

Who are the scornful? Scoffers and mockers of God and His Son.

Therefore, this means the man who prospers *will:*

1. *Walk* in the counsel of the godly.

2. *Stand* in the way of the righteous.

3. *Sit* in the seat of those who edify.

God is not against using positive messages too:

> **But his delight is in the law of the Lord; and in his law doth he meditate day and night.**
>
> **And he shall be like a tree planted by the rivers of water, that bringeth forth his fruit in his season; his leaf also shall not wither; *and whatsoever he doeth shall prosper.***
>
> **Psalm 1:2-3**

TIP #2
Memorize Joshua 1:8 and Psalm 1:1–3 and quote them constantly around the house, on the way to work each morning and before you go to sleep at night. Then memorize one scripture per week from those found in this book. Constantly speak these scriptures over and over. Within one year you will have committed over 50 Scriptures to memory, in two years 100, in five years 500. You will be amazed with the results.

In the book of Deuteronomy, we find much about success and prosperity. Deuteronomy is basically a summary of Exodus, Leviticus, and Numbers, yet it contains a detailed list of blessings for following God's Word. Let us hear the words of Moses as he recounts the Abrahamic covenant.

And it shall come to pass, if thou shalt hearken diligently unto the voice of the Lord thy God, to observe and to do all his commandments which I command thee this day, that the Lord thy God will set thee on high above all nations of the earth:

And all these blessings shall come on thee, and overtake thee, if thou shalt hearken unto the voice of the Lord thy God.

Blessed shalt thou be in the city, and blessed shalt thou be in the field.

Blessed shall be the fruit of thy body, and the fruit of thy ground, and the fruit of thy cattle, the increase of thy kine, and the flocks of thy sheep.

Blessed shall be thy basket and thy store.

Blessed shalt thou be when thou comest in, and blessed shalt thou be when thou goest out.

The Lord shall cause thine enemies that rise up against thee to be smitten before thy face: they shall come out against thee one way, and flee before thee seven ways.

The Lord shall command the blessing upon thee in thy storehouses, and in all that thou settest thine hand unto; and he shall bless thee in the land which the Lord thy God giveth thee.

The Lord shall establish thee an holy people unto himself, as he hath sworn unto thee, if thou shalt keep the commandments of the Lord thy God, and walk in his ways.

And all people of the earth shall see that thou art called by the name of the Lord; and they shall be afraid of thee.

13

And the Lord shall make thee plenteous in goods, in the fruit of thy body, and in the fruit of thy cattle, and in the fruit of thy ground, in the land which the Lord sware unto thy fathers to give thee.

The Lord shall open unto thee his good treasure, the heaven to give the rain unto thy land in his season, and to bless all the work of thine hand: and thou shalt lend unto many nations, and thou shalt not borrow.

And the Lord shall make thee the head, and not the tail; and thou shalt be above only, and thou shalt not be beneath; if that thou hearken unto the commandments of the Lord thy God, which I command thee this day, to observe and to do them.

Deuteronomy 28:1-13

Some people in the church try to "spiritualize" away these blessings with confusing rhetoric and allegories. However, the blessings of God should be taken quite literally. In many places in God's Word we do find symbolic meanings and double references but that does not mean that God's Word and promises are not to be taken literally!

We also learn later in Deuteronomy that God's Word is not hidden nor is it hard to understand as some people try to make us think.

For this commandment which I command thee this day, *it is not hidden from thee, neither is it far off.*

It is not in heaven, that thou shouldest say, Who shall go up for us to heaven, and bring it unto us, that we may hear it, and do it?

Neither is it beyond the sea, that thou shouldest say, Who shall go over the sea for us, and bring it unto us, that we may hear it, and do it?

But the word is very nigh unto thee, in thy mouth, and in thy heart, thou mayest do it.

See, I have set before thee this day life and good, and death and evil;

In that I command thee this day to love the Lord thy God, to walk in his ways, and to keep his commandments and his statutes, and his judgments, that thou mayest live and multiply: and *the Lord thy God shall bless thee in the land whither thou goest to possess it.*

Deuteronomy 30:11-16

If we continue to read from the above passage and skip to verse 19 and 20, we see that people all over the world and down through the ages have had to make the same choice—life or death, blessing or cursing. Everyone gets to use their *free will* to make that choice. God did not design us as robots but as free moral agents. However, God does gives us a very powerful suggestion. He recommends that we choose life.

I call heaven and earth to record this day against you, that *I have set before you life and death, blessing and cursing: therefore choose life,* that both thou and thy seed may live:

That thou mayest love the Lord thy God, and that thou mayest obey his voice, and that thou mayest cleave unto him: for he is thy life, and the length of thy days: that thou mayest dwell in the land which the Lord sware unto thy fathers, to Abraham, to Isaac, and to Jacob, to give them.

Deuteronomy 30:19-20

The last few scriptures that we've been looking at have come from the book of Deuteronomy. Deuteronomy is the fifth book of our Bible and contains much on the subject of wealth and blessings. It also happens to be the last book of the Torah (the Torah contains the first five books of the Bible, written by Moses). Some scholars believe that this book alone (not the whole Torah) was put inside the Ark of the Covenant.

And it came to pass, when Moses had made an end of writing the words of this law in a book, until they were finished,

That Moses commanded the Levites, which bare the ark of the covenant of the Lord, saying,

> **Take this book of the law, and put it in the side of the ark of the covenant of the Lord your God, that it may be there for a witness against thee.**
>
> Deuteronomy 31:24-26

God inspired Moses to give instructions that the book of Deuteronomy was to be placed alongside the Ten Commandments inside the Ark of the Covenant. During the reign of King Josiah, this book was found in the house of the Lord by Hilkiah, the High Priest.

> **And Hilkiah the high priest said unto Shaphan the scribe,** *I have found the book of the law in the house of the Lord.* **And Hilkiah gave the book to Shaphan, and he read it.**
>
> **2 Kings 22:8**

From the account of 2 Kings 22 and 23 it seems evident from the reforms of Josiah that Deuteronomy was the book that was found.

> **Now the king sent them to gather all the elders of Judah and Jerusalem to him.**
>
> **The king went up to the house of the Lord with all the men of Judah, and with him all the inhabitants of Jerusalem— the priests and the prophets and all the people, both small and great. And he read in their hearing all the words of the Book of the Covenant which had been found in the house of the Lord.**
>
> **Then the king stood by a pillar and made a covenant before the Lord, to follow the Lord and to keep His commandments and His testimonies and His statutes, with all his heart and all his soul, to perform the words of this covenant that were written in this book. And all the people took a stand for the covenant.**
>
> **2 Kings 23:1-3 (NKJV)**

Josiah restored true worship and encouraged the people to take a stand for the Covenant (the Word of God). Now, when we come to New Testament times, we find a very interesting discovery. The first three scriptures Jesus quoted were all from the book of Deuteronomy!

And Jesus being full of the Holy Ghost returned from Jordan, and was led by the Spirit into the wilderness,

Being forty days tempted of the devil. And in those days he did eat nothing: and when they were ended, he afterward hungered.

And the devil said unto him, If thou be the Son of God, command this stone that it be made bread.

And Jesus answered him, saying, It is written, *That man shall not live by bread alone, but by every word of God* (Deuteronomy 8:3.)

And the devil, taking him up into an high mountain, shewed unto him all the kingdoms of the world in a moment of time.

And the devil said unto him, All this power will I give thee, and the glory of them: for that is delivered unto me; and to whomsoever I will I give it.

If thou therefore wilt worship me, all shall be thine.

And Jesus answered and said unto him, Get thee behind me, Satan: for it is written, *Thou shalt worship the Lord thy God, and him only shalt thou serve* (Deuteronomy 6:13.)

And he brought him to Jerusalem, and set him on a pinnacle of the temple, and said unto him, If thou be the Son of God, cast thyself down from hence:

For it is written, He shall give his angels charge over thee, to keep thee:

And in their hands they shall bear thee up, lest at any time thou dash thy foot against a stone.

And Jesus answering said unto him, It is said, *Thou shalt not tempt the Lord thy God.* (Deuteronomy 6:16.)

And when the devil had ended all the temptation, he departed from him for a season.

And Jesus returned in the power of the Spirit into Galilee: and there went out a fame of him through all the region round about.

And he taught in their synagogues, being glorified of all.

Luke 4:1-15

17

Jesus validated the contents of the book of Deuteronomy when He quoted from this book at the start of His ministry. It is also interesting to note that the original Hebrew title of Deuteronomy is *Devarim* which in English is the plural for "The Word." In the gospel of John, we see that Jesus is also called "The Word" (*logos* in Greek).

Since Moses wrote Deuteronomy and Jesus first quoted from it, let's look at some other passages from this glorious book.

> But thou shalt remember the Lord thy God: *for it is he that giveth thee power to get wealth,* that he may establish his covenant which he sware unto thy fathers, as it is this day.
>
> Deuteronomy 8:18
>
> And all these blessings shall come on thee, and overtake thee, if thou shalt hearken unto the voice of the Lord thy God.
>
> Blessed shalt thou be in the city, and blessed shalt thou be in the field.
>
> Blessed shall be the fruit of thy body, and the fruit of thy ground, and the fruit of thy cattle, the increase of thy kine, and the flocks of thy sheep.
>
> Blessed shall be thy basket and thy store. Blessed shalt thou be when thou comest in, and blessed shalt thou be when thou goest out.
>
> The Lord shall cause thine enemies that rise up against thee to be smitten before thy face: they shall come out against thee one way, and flee before thee seven ways.
>
> The Lord shall command the blessing upon thee in thy storehouses, and in all that thou settest thine hand unto; and he shall bless thee in the land which the Lord thy God giveth thee.
>
> Deuteronomy 28:2-8
>
> The Lord shall open unto thee his good treasure, the heaven to give the rain unto thy land in his season,

**and to bless all the work of thine hand: and thou shalt
lend unto many nations, and thou shalt not borrow.**

**And the Lord shall make thee the head, and not the
tail; and thou shalt be above only, and thou shalt not be
beneath; if that thou hearken unto the commandments
of the Lord thy God, which I command thee this day, to
observe and to do them:**

Deuteronomy 28:12-13

One man who achieved great success and wealth was
Abraham. While he inherited many spiritual blessings, he
was physically blessed too.

**And Abram was very rich in cattle, in silver, and in
gold.**

Genesis 13:2

Abraham is a perfect example that you can never be too
old to serve God.

Joseph was another man who was prosperous and
successful. However, Joseph's life shows young people that
you can never be too young to serve God, since he became
"second in command" over all of Egypt at 30 years of age.
Let's look at Joseph in Genesis 39:2 both from the *King James
Version* and the *New King James Version.*

**And the Lord was with Joseph, and *he was a
prosperous man;* and he was in the house of his master
the Egyptian.**

Genesis 39:2

**The Lord was with Joseph, and *he was a successful
man;* and he was in the house of his master the Egyptian.**

Genesis 39:2 (NKJV)

Sounds great, but all of those scriptures are from the
Old Testament. Okay, let's take a look at some New
Testament scriptures too. The next passage is long but it is
very important. It shows that all believers have their
heritage (or roots) in Abraham.

**Even as Abraham believed God, and it was
accounted to him for righteousness.**

Know ye therefore that they which are of faith, the same are the children of Abraham.

And the scripture, foreseeing that God would justify the heathen through faith, preached before the gospel unto Abraham, saying, In thee shall all nations be blessed.

So then they which be of faith are blessed with faithful Abraham.

For as many as are of the works of the law are under the curse: for it is written, Cursed is every one that continueth not in all things which are written in the book of the law to do them.

But that no man is justified by the law in the sight of God, it is evident: for, The just shall live by faith.

And the law is not of faith: but, The man that doeth them shall live in them.

Christ hath redeemed us from the curse of the law, being made a curse for us: for it is written, Cursed is every one that hangeth on a tree:

That the blessing of Abraham might come on the Gentiles through Jesus Christ; that we might receive the promise of the Spirit through faith.

Brethren, I speak after the manner of men; Though it be but a man's covenant, yet if it be confirmed, no man disannulleth, or addeth thereto.

Now to Abraham and his seed were the promises made. He saith not, And to seeds, as of many; but as of one, And to thy seed, which is Christ.

And this I say, that the covenant, that was confirmed before of God in Christ, the law, which was four hundred and thirty years after, cannot disannul, that it should make the promise of none effect.

For if the inheritance be of the law, it is no more of promise: but God gave it to Abraham by promise.

Wherefore then serveth the law? It was added because of transgressions, till the seed should come to whom the promise was made; and it was ordained by angels in the hand of a mediator.

Now a mediator is not a mediator of one, but God is one.

Is the law then against the promises of God? God forbid: for if there had been a law given which could have given life, verily righteousness should have been by the law.

But the scripture hath concluded all under sin, that the promise by faith of Jesus Christ might be given to them that believe.

But before faith came, we were kept under the law, shut up unto the faith which should afterwards be revealed.

Wherefore the law was our schoolmaster to bring us unto Christ, that we might be justified by faith.

But after that faith is come, we are no longer under a schoolmaster.

For ye are all the children of God by faith in Christ Jesus.

For as many of you as have been baptized into Christ have put on Christ.

There is neither Jew nor Greek, there is neither bond nor free, there is neither male nor female: for ye are all one in Christ Jesus.

And if ye be Christ's, then are ye Abraham's seed, and heirs according to the promise.

Galatians 3:6-29

Jesus Christ has done away with the curse of the law. ("The curse" is poverty, sickness, disease, and separation from God.) However, as the third chapter of Galatians states, the blessings and promises to Abraham are still in effect if you belong to Jesus Christ!

And if ye be Christ's, then are ye Abraham's seed, and "heirs" according to the promise.

Galatians 3:29

Remember that Joshua said for biblical prosperity and success we must begin by doing three things, which are the subjects of the next three chapters.

21

Speak the Word (chapter 2)

Meditate on the Word day and night (chapter 3)

Observe and Do according to the Word (chapter 4)

Another passage from the New Testament reveals some very interesting comments regarding prosperity in three important areas: material prosperity (wealth), physical prosperity (health), and our spiritual prosperity (relationship with God).

> **Beloved, I pray that you may prosper in all things and be in health, just as your soul prospers.**
> **3 John 2 (NKJV)**

Is this a "Health and Wealth Gospel"? You better believe it! But don't forget the most important aspect of all, *your salvation!*

> **For what shall it profit a man, if he shall gain the whole world, and lose his own soul?**
> **Mark 8:36**

Health and wealth won't do you much good in the long term if you're headed for the wrong place in the near term. However, if your relationship with God and your eternal destination are secure, then you just continue praying and believing 3 John 2. *It was written just for you!*

> **Beloved, I pray that you may prosper in all things and be in health, just as your soul prospers.**
> **3 John 2 (NKJV)**

It can't be more clear than that. Health, wealth, and spiritual prosperity are just for you! It is guaranteed by both the Old and New Testaments. Listen to the benefits of God's divine prosperity plan.

> **Bless the Lord, O my soul, and forget not all his benefits:**
> **Who forgiveth all thine iniquities; who healeth all thy diseases;**
> **Who redeemeth thy life from destruction; who crowneth thee with lovingkindness and tender mercies;**

Who satisfieth thy mouth with good things; so that thy youth is renewed like the eagle's.

The Lord executeth righteousness and judgment for all that are oppressed.

He made known his ways unto Moses, his acts unto the children of Israel.

The Lord is merciful and gracious, slow to anger, and plenteous in mercy.

He will not always chide: neither will he keep his anger for ever.

He hath not dealt with us after our sins; nor rewarded us according to our iniquities.

For as the heaven is high above the earth, so great is his mercy toward them that fear him.

As far as the east is from the west, so far hath he removed our transgressions from us.

Like as a father pitieth his children, so the Lord pitieth them that fear him.

For he knoweth our frame; he remembereth that we are dust.

As for man, his days are as grass: as a flower of the field, so he flourisheth.

For the wind passeth over it, and it is gone; and the place thereof shall know it no more.

But the mercy of the Lord is from everlasting to everlasting upon them that fear him, and his righteousness unto children's children;

To such as keep his covenant, and to those that remember his commandments to do them.

The Lord hath prepared his throne in the heavens; and his kingdom ruleth over all.

Bless the Lord, ye his angels, that excel in strength, that do his commandments, hearkening unto the voice of his word.

Bless ye the Lord, all ye his hosts; ye ministers of his, that do his pleasure.

Bless the Lord, all his works in all places of his
dominion: bless the Lord, O my soul.

Psalm 103:2-22

TIP #3

Turn off the car radio! Begin listening to teaching
and preaching tapes from ministries that are based on
the Word of God. You can literally receive an "ongoing
education on wheels" while driving your car, sitting in
traffic jams, and waiting at stoplights. You will rarely
turn your radio on again after you see how much
wisdom and knowledge you can gain during your
driving time.

Success, prosperity, and abundant life. These are all
promises in God's Word. For further verification, let's look
at the words of Jesus.

I am the door: by me if any man enter in, he shall be
saved, and shall go in and out, and find pasture.

The thief cometh not, but for to steal, and to kill,
and to destroy: *I am come that they might have life, and
that they might have it more abundantly.*

I am the good shepherd: the good shepherd giveth
his life for the sheep.

John 10:9-11

Notice that there is a thief, an adversary. His name is
Satan. There was not much revelation about him in the Old
Testament but the New Testament makes it quite clear.
Satan is the one who comes to kill, steal, and destroy while
Jesus comes to give *life more abundantly.* Not just abundantly,
but *more abundantly*! Too many people confuse the works of
Satan, who brings death and destruction, with the works of
God, Who brings healing, help, restoration, and the promise
of abundant life. If you've had problems understanding the
book of Job or maybe tragedies in your own life, then look
through the eyes of the New Testament to understand the
methods of Satan compared to the attributes of God.

Jesus made it very clear that He came to do the will of the Father.

How God anointed Jesus of Nazareth with the Holy Ghost and with power: who went about doing good, and *healing all that were oppressed of the devil;* for God was with him.

Acts 10:38

Forasmuch then as the children are partakers of flesh and blood, he also himself likewise took part of the same; *that through death he might destroy him that had the power of death, that is, the devil.*

Hebrews 2:14

To open their eyes, and to turn them from darkness to light, and from the power of Satan unto God, that they may receive forgiveness of sins, and inheritance among them which are sanctified by faith that is in me.

Acts 26:18

Who hath *delivered us from the power of darkness,* and hath translated us into the kingdom of his dear Son.

Colossians 1:13

Little children, let no man deceive you: he that doeth righteousness is righteous, even as he is righteous.

He that committeth sin is of the devil; for the devil sinneth from the beginning. *For this purpose the Son of God was manifested, that he might destroy the works of the devil.*

1 John 3:7-8

True success will be just beyond your reach until you understand who is the "destroyer" and Who is the "Restorer."

The bombing of the Murrah Federal Building in Oklahoma City is one such example. Many people think that God was responsible for the bombing since He "allowed it." The only thing that God allows to happen is for people to make choices. Unfortunately, many people allow themselves to be influenced by Satan which in turn causes innocent people to suffer. Jesus revealed the Father to us. Nowhere in the New Testament do you find Jesus stealing, killing, or destroying people. Religious tradition often teaches one thing while the Word of God teaches something quite different. Discover who is the real culprit behind the evil of a man's heart. Only then can you wage an effective war against your adversary.

Let's look again at John 10:10.

> **The thief cometh not, but for to steal, and to kill, and to destroy: I am come that they might have life, and that they might have it more *abundantly*.**
>
> **John 10:10**

What is this abundant life that Jesus is talking about? Since we already understand what life is, let's look at the meaning of the Greek word for *abundant* in *Strong's Concordance*:

> *4053 perissos (per-is-sos'); from 4012 (in the sense of beyond); superabundant (in quantity) or superior (in quality); by implication, excessive; adverbially (with 1537) violently; neuter (as noun) preeminence; KJV— exceeding abundantly above, more abundantly, advantage, exceedingly, very highly, beyond measure, more, superfluous, vehement [-ly].*

Paul also used this word when he wrote to the church at Ephesus.

> **And to know the love of Christ, which passeth knowledge, that ye might be filled with all the fulness of God. Now unto him that is able to do exceeding *abundantly* above all that we ask or think, according to the power that worketh in us.**
>
> **Ephesians 3:19-20**

26

Exceeding abundantly above all that we can ask or think! This is the amount of success, prosperity, and abundant life promised to you by God's Word, conditioned upon Joshua 1:8. "But what about the poor?" The promises of the Bible are for everyone!

What did you think Jesus meant by bringing the "good news to the poor"?

> The Spirit of the Lord is upon me, because *he hath anointed me to preach the gospel to the poor;* he hath sent me to heal the brokenhearted, to preach deliverance to the captives, and recovering of sight to the blind, to set at liberty them that are bruised,
>
> To preach the acceptable year of the Lord.
>
> **Luke 4:18-19**

The gospel or "The Good News" to the poor is *that they don't have to be poor anymore!* Isn't that good news?

But what about those scriptures that warn against having or chasing after riches? And what about money being the root of all evil?

> Do not overwork to be rich; because of your own understanding, cease!
>
> Will you set your eyes on that which is not? For riches certainly make themselves wings; they fly away like an eagle toward heaven.
>
> **Proverbs 23:4-5 (NKJV)**
>
> He also that received seed among the thorns is he that heareth the word; and the care of this world, and *the deceitfulness of riches,* choke the word, and he becometh unfruitful.
>
> **Matthew 13:22**
>
> For *the love of money* is the root of all evil: which while some coveted after, they have erred from the faith, and pierced themselves through with many sorrows.
>
> **1 Timothy 6:10**

> **Charge them that are rich in this world, that they be not highminded, *nor trust in uncertain riches*, but in the living God, who giveth us richly all things to enjoy;**
>
> **That they do good, that they be rich in good works, ready to distribute, willing to communicate.**
>
> **1 Timothy 6:17-18**

It is not riches that are cautioned against in God's Word, it is the *deceitfulness* of them. It's not the money itself that is bad, it is the *love* of money that is evil. Do you see the difference between the traditional interpretations of men and what the Word of God actually says? Money and riches are neither good nor bad. They can be used for good or for evil. A rich person who oppresses the poor or spends his money on riotous living is obviously not in line with God's Word. However, a rich person who gives generously into the kingdom of God is in line with God's Word. Money can be spent on drugs or it can be used to spread the gospel. *People are the ones who are either good or bad, not the money itself!*

Proverbs 28:20 distinguishes between these two groups of people.

> **A faithful man shall abound with blessings: but he that maketh haste to be rich shall not be innocent.**

Sometimes there is a temptation to feel condemned once you've discovered that it is not God's will for you to be poor. Don't feel condemned if your finances are not where the Word promises they can be. Instead, make some changes in your life but refuse to accept the condemnation of the enemy.

> **There is therefore now no condemnation to them which are in Christ Jesus, who walk not after the flesh, but after the Spirit.**
>
> **Romans 8:1**

However, Romans 8:1 also reminds us not to accept the condemnation of those who reject God's message of prosperity and success. Those who don't want you to prosper and succeed are usually people who have never prospered or succeeded in life themselves. Their self–image will be tarnished further if they see you start walking in the blessings of the Lord. Why listen or take advice from these people? Matthew 15:14 says, **If the blind leads the blind, both will fall into the ditch!** It is easy to stay out of the ditch if you listen to God's Word instead of man's words. We'll discuss this later in another chapter.

Let's conclude by looking at a few more scriptures from the book of Proverbs.

> **I love those who love me, and those who seek me diligently will find me.**
>
> *Riches and honor are with me, enduring riches and righteousness.*
>
> **My fruit is better than gold, yes, than fine gold, and my revenue than choice silver.**
>
> **I traverse the way of righteousness, in the midst of the paths of justice,**
>
> *That I may cause those who love me to inherit wealth, that I may fill their treasuries.*
>
> **Proverbs 8:17-21 (NKJV)**
>
> **Treasures of wickedness profit nothing: but righteousness delivereth from death.**
>
> **The Lord will not suffer the soul of the righteous to famish: but he casteth away the substance of the wicked.**
>
> **He becometh poor that dealeth with a slack hand: *but the hand of the diligent maketh rich.***
>
> *The blessing of the Lord, it maketh rich, and he addeth no sorrow with it.*
>
> **Proverbs 10:2-4,22**

The Word of God is very clear when it comes to prosperity and success. Doubters and unbelievers obviously haven't spent enough time in the Word to realize that man's traditions of poverty are simply untrue and have no scriptural basis. In fact, it has been an outright satanic plot to keep the Body of Christ in such a state of poverty that the spread of the gospel would be hindered. However, this has already begun to change. The Word is out. God is true and the enemy is a liar!

Throughout the rest of this book we will continue to let the Word of God be our guide. The Word will show us how we can obtain what God has promised, so that we may do what He has already commissioned.

CHAPTER 2
SPEAKING THE WORD

> But the word is very nigh unto thee, *in thy mouth,*
> and in thy heart, that thou mayest do it.
>
> Deuteronomy 30:14

What does it mean to "speak the Word"? Isn't that just quoting scripture? There is a big difference between just "quoting scripture" and "speaking the Word of God." Let's examine several scriptures to get a better idea of this first prerequisite of godly success.

> And these words, which I command thee this day,
> shall be in thine heart:
>
> And thou shalt teach them diligently unto thy
> children, and *shalt talk of them when thou sittest in
> thine house, and when thou walkest by the way, and
> when thou liest down, and when thou risest up.*
>
> And thou shalt bind them for a sign upon thine
> hand, and they shall be as frontlets between thine eyes.
>
> And thou shalt write them upon the posts of thy
> house, and on thy gates.
>
> Deuteronomy 6:6-9

> When all Israel is come to appear before the Lord
> thy God in the place which he shall choose, *thou shalt
> read this law before all Israel in their hearing.*
>
> Deuteronomy 31:11

> *The mouth of the righteous speaketh wisdom, and
> his tongue talketh of judgment.*
>
> The law of his God is in his heart; none of his steps
> shall slide.
>
> Psalm 37:30-31

I have not hid thy righteousness within my heart; *I have declared thy faithfulness and thy salvation: I have not concealed thy lovingkindness and thy truth from the great congregation.*

Psalm 40:10

So shall I have wherewith *to answer him that reproacheth me*: for I trust in thy word.

And take not the word of truth utterly out of my mouth; for I have hoped in thy judgments.

Psalm 119:42-43

As for me, this is my covenant with them, saith the Lord; My spirit that is upon thee, and *my words which I have put in thy mouth,* shall not depart out of thy mouth, nor out of the mouth of thy seed, nor out of the mouth of thy seed's seed, saith the Lord, from henceforth and for ever.

Isaiah 59:21

Acquaint now thyself with him, and be at peace: thereby good shall come unto thee.

Receive, I pray thee, the law from his mouth, and lay up his words in thine heart.

If thou return to the Almighty, thou shalt be built up, thou shalt put away iniquity far from thy tabernacles.

Then shalt thou lay up gold as dust, and the gold of Ophir as the stones of the brooks.

Yea, the Almighty shall be thy defense, and thou shalt have plenty of silver.

For then shalt thou have thy delight in the Almighty, and shalt lift up thy face unto God.

Thou shalt make thy prayer unto him, and he shall hear thee, and thou shalt pay thy vows.

Thou shalt also decree a thing, and it shall be established unto thee: and the light shall shine upon thy ways.

Job 22:21-28

A good man out of the good treasure of the heart bringeth forth good things: and an evil man out of the evil treasure bringeth forth evil things.

Matthew 12:35

Let us hold fast the *profession of our faith* without wavering; (for he is faithful that promised.)

Hebrews 10:23

Let no corrupt communication proceed out of your mouth, but that which is good to the use of edifying, that it may minister grace unto the hearers.

Ephesians 4:29

Not only is speaking the Word very important, those scriptures just listed show us *how important all of our words are!* Words have the power to heal, to encourage, and to bless others. Unfortunately, words also have the power to destroy, to slander, and to curse. The Word (strange how we call the Bible "the Word") teaches us the power that our words command. In the book of Proverbs, Solomon writes:

***Death and life are in the power of the tongue:* and they that love it shall eat the fruit thereof.**

Proverbs 18:21

The above scripture simply means, those who love to use their words (whether for good or bad) will bear the consequences of the things they say. James also gives us a detailed account of those who aren't right with God and their uncontrollable words.

Behold, we put bits in the horses' mouths, that they may obey us; and we turn about their whole body.

Behold also the ships, which though they be so great, and are driven of fierce winds, yet are they turned about with a very small helm, whithersoever the governor listeth.

Even so the tongue is a little member, and boasteth great things. Behold, how great a matter a little fire kindleth!

***And the tongue is a fire, a world of iniquity:* so is the tongue among our members, that it defileth the whole**

body, and setteth on fire the course of nature; and it is set on fire of hell.

For every kind of beasts, and of birds, and of serpents, and of things in the sea, is tamed, and hath been tamed of mankind:

But the tongue can no man tame; it is an unruly evil, full of deadly poison.

Therewith bless we God, even the Father; and therewith curse we men, which are made after the similitude of God.

Out of the same mouth proceedeth blessing and cursing. My brethren, these things ought not so to be.

Doth a fountain send forth at the same place sweet water and bitter?

Can the fig tree, my brethren, bear olive berries? either a vine, figs? so can no fountain both yield salt water and fresh.

Who is a wise man and endued with knowledge among you? let him shew out of a good conversation his works with meekness of wisdom.

James 3:3-13

Look back at verse 6, "and setteth on fire the course of *nature.*"

The word *nature* here in *Strong's Concordance* comes from the Greek word *genesis.* (#5449.) Isn't that amazing? James teaches how negative words can change the course of *nature* while God in the book of *Genesis* demonstrates how positive words can also change the course of nature.

And God said, Let there be light: *and there was light.*

And God saw the light, that it was good: and God divided the light from the darkness.

And God called the light Day, and the darkness he called Night. And the evening and the morning were the first day

And God said, Let there be a firmament in the midst of the waters, and let it divide the waters from the waters.

And God made the firmament, and divided the waters which were under the firmament from the waters which were above the firmament: *and it was so.*

And God called the firmament Heaven. And the evening and the morning were the second day.

And God said, Let the waters under the heaven be gathered together unto one place, and let the dry land appear: *and it was so.*

And God called the dry land Earth; and the gathering together of the waters called he Seas: and God saw that it was good.

And God said, Let the earth bring forth grass, the herb yielding seed, and the fruit tree yielding fruit after his kind, whose seed is in itself, upon the earth: *and it was so.*

And the earth brought forth grass, and herb yielding seed after his kind, and the tree yielding fruit, whose seed was in itself, after his kind: and God saw that it was good.

And the evening and the morning were the third day.

And God said, Let there be lights in the firmament of the heaven to divide the day from the night; and let them be for signs, and for seasons, and for days, and years:

And let them be for lights in the firmament of the heaven to give light upon the earth: *and it was so.*

And God made two great lights; the greater light to rule the day, and the lesser light to rule the night: he made the stars also.

And God set them in the firmament of the heaven to give light upon the earth,

And to rule over the day and over the night, and to divide the light from the darkness: and God saw that it was good.

And the evening and the morning were the fourth day.

And God said, Let the waters bring forth abundantly the moving creature that hath life, and fowl that may fly above the earth in the open firmament of heaven.

And God created great whales, and every living creature that moveth, which the waters brought forth abundantly, after their kind, and every winged fowl after his kind: and God saw that it was good.

And God blessed them, saying, Be fruitful, and multiply, and fill the waters in the seas, and let fowl multiply in the earth.

And the evening and the morning were the fifth day.

And God said, Let the earth bring forth the living creature after his kind, cattle, and creeping thing, and beast of the earth after his kind: *and it was so.*

And God made the beast of the earth after his kind, and cattle after their kind, and every thing that creepeth upon the earth after his kind: and God saw that it was good.

And God said, Let us make man in our image, after our likeness: and let them have dominion over the fish of the sea, and over the fowl of the air, and over the cattle, and over all the earth, and over every creeping thing that creepeth upon the earth.

So God created man in his own image, in the image of God created he him; male and female created he them.

And God blessed them, *and God said unto them,* Be fruitful, and multiply, and replenish the earth, and subdue it: and have dominion over the fish of the sea, and over the fowl of the air, and over every living thing that moveth upon the earth.

And God said, Behold, I have given you every herb bearing seed, which is upon the face of all the earth, and every tree, in the which is the fruit of a tree yielding seed; to you it shall be for meat.

Genesis 1:3–31

Thus the heavens and the earth were finished, and all the host of them.

Genesis 2:1

Before God created anything, he spoke it first. "And God said," "And God said," "And God said," "And God said."

The book of Hebrews also sheds light on this subject.

Now faith is the substance of things hoped for, the evidence of things not seen.

For by it the elders obtained a good report.

Through faith we understand that the worlds were framed by *the word of God*, so that things which are seen were not made of things which do appear.

Hebrews 11:1-3

The italicized words, "the word of God," is actually a play on words. Not only were the worlds created by the "words of God," they were created by *the Word* (which is another name for Jesus Christ). This title was used only by the apostle John.

In the beginning was the Word, and the Word was with God, and the Word was God.

The same was in the beginning with God.

All things were made by him; and without him was not any thing made that was made.

In him was life; and the life was the light of men.

And the light shineth in darkness; and the darkness comprehended it not....

...That was the true Light, which lighteth every man that cometh into the world.

He was in the world, and the world was made by him, and the world knew him not.

He came unto his own, and his own received him not.

But as many as received him, to them gave he power to become the sons of God, even to them that believe on his name:

Which were born, not of blood, nor of the will of the flesh, nor of the will of man, but of God.

And the Word was made flesh, and dwelt among us, (and we beheld his glory, the glory as of the only begotten of the Father,) full of grace and truth.

John bare witness of him, and cried, saying, This was he of whom I spake, He that cometh after me is preferred before me: for he was before me.

And of his fulness have all we received, and grace for grace. For the law was given by Moses, but grace and truth came by Jesus Christ.

John 1:1-16

Note the similarities between the first chapter of Genesis and the first chapter of John's gospel. In Genesis, God's "words" created everything. In John's gospel it says "The Word" (Jesus Christ) made all things. Hebrews also reinforces this message.

God, who at sundry times and in divers manners spake in time past unto the fathers by the prophets,

Hath in these last days spoken unto us by his Son, whom he hath appointed heir of all things, by whom also he made the worlds;

Who being the brightness of his glory, and the express image of his person, *and upholding all things by the word of his power,* when he had by himself purged our sins, sat down on the right hand of the Majesty on high.

Hebrews 1:1-3

Since it is very clear that God's Words are important, we must realize how important our words are too.

Death and life are in the power of the tongue: and they that love it shall eat the fruit thereof.

Proverbs 18:21

Therefore, as the psalmist says:

Set a watch, O Lord, before my mouth; keep the door of my lips.

Psalm 141:3

> **Tip #4**
>
> For the next several days, pay close attention to the words you say and listen closely to the conversations of other people. Count how many times your hear people say these things. "That just thrilled me to death," "Scared me to death," "I'm just dying to go," "I'm so unlucky," "Think I'm coming down with something," and other negative sayings. You'll be amazed. For further study, Kenneth Hagin, Charles Capps, Kenneth Copeland, and Jerry Savelle have some of the best teachings on the words that we speak and the power they command. Order some tapes from these men and learn how to speak in accordance with God's Word instead of the world's way. You can literally change the course of events in your life, but it will have to start with the words that you speak to yourself and others.

In the gospel of Matthew we hear Jesus teaching about our words.

Not that which goeth into the mouth defileth a man; but that which cometh out of the mouth, this defileth a man.

Then came his disciples, and said unto him, Knowest thou that the Pharisees were offended, after they heard this saying?

But he answered and said, Every plant, which my heavenly Father hath not planted, shall be rooted up.

Let them alone: they be blind leaders of the blind. And if the blind lead the blind, both shall fall into the ditch.

Then answered Peter and said unto him, Declare unto us this parable.

And Jesus said, Are ye also yet without understanding?

Do not ye yet understand, that whatsoever entereth in at the mouth goeth into the belly, and is cast out into the draught?

But those things which proceed out of the mouth come forth from the heart; and they defile the man.

For out of the heart proceed evil thoughts, murders, adulteries, fornications, thefts, false witness, blasphemies:

These are the things which defile a man: but to eat with unwashen hands defileth not a man.

Matthew 15:11-20

But I say unto you, That every idle word that men shall speak, they shall give account thereof in the day of judgment.

Matthew 12:36

The next time you get ready to give someone "a piece of your mind" for something they did, think about this scripture and choose to be silent. Be determined to excel in this first step of success and make sure everything that comes out of your mouth is in line with God's Word.

Seest thou a man that is hasty in his words? there is more hope of a fool than of him.

Proverbs 29:20

40

CHAPTER 3
MEDITATING ON THE WORD

We just learned how to "speak the Word," but we meditate on the Word by *reading, pondering, studying, memorizing,* and *praying* God's Word. Let's look at several scriptures that have to do with this aspect of achieving greater success.

But his delight is in the law of the Lord; and in his law doth he *meditate* day and night.

And he shall be like a tree planted by the rivers of water, that bringeth forth his fruit in his season; his leaf also shall not wither; and whatsoever he doeth shall prosper.

Psalm 1:2-3

Let the words of my mouth, and the *meditation* of my heart, be acceptable in thy sight, O Lord, my strength, and my redeemer.

Psalm 19:14

Thy word have I *hid* in mine heart, that I might not sin against thee.

Psalm 119:11

I will *meditate* in thy precepts, and have respect unto thy ways.

Psalm 119:15

O how love I thy law! it is my *meditation* all the day.

Psalm 119:97

I have more understanding than all my teachers: for thy testimonies are my *meditation.*

Psalm 119:99

My son, if thou wilt receive my words, and *hide* my commandments with thee;

So that thou incline thine ear unto wisdom, and apply thine heart to understanding;

Yea, if thou criest after knowledge, and liftest up thy voice for understanding;

If thou seekest her as silver, and searchest for her as for hid treasures; then shalt thou understand the fear of the Lord, and find the knowledge of God.

Proverbs 2:1-5

My son, forget not my law; but let thine heart keep my commandments.

Proverbs 3:1

Neglect not the gift that is in thee, which was given thee by prophecy, with the laying on of the hands of the presbytery.

Meditate upon these things; give thyself wholly to them; that thy profiting may appear to all.

Take heed unto thyself, and unto the doctrine; continue in them: for in doing this thou shalt both save thyself, and them that hear thee.

1 Timothy 4:14-16

The word *meditate* appears often in these scriptures. Turn to your *Strong's Concordance* as we discover the meaning of this word in Hebrew. The Hebrew word for meditate is *hagah* pronounced "haw–gaw." It means to *murmur (in pleasure or anger); by implication, to ponder, imagine, meditate, mourn, mutter, roar, speak, study, talk, or utter* (#1897).

The word *meditation* often has connotations of the New Age or of eastern religions. Add to it the thoughts of imagination, concentration, and visualization and most Bible–believing Christians are ready to escort you out the door. However, all of these terms originated in God's Word and were meant for His people as they study His Word. Most New Age teachings are not new at all but rather are a perversion of God's Word.

TIP #5

As Psalm 1:2 says, "And *in his law doth he meditate day and night.*" The power that you will receive in your life by following his advice is immeasurable. In addition to your daily study of God's Word, spend your very first waking moments in the Word and again right before you go to sleep every single day of your life. You will be amazed at the outcome if you make this a part of your daily routine. Just as you feed your body with food each day to sustain physical life, you need to realize how important it is to feed your spirit each day with God's Word.

Meditating on God's Word is crucial for success. God's Word is your eternal guide and the substance that feeds your spirit.

Thy word is a lamp unto my feet, and a light unto my path.

Psalm 119:105

But he answered and said, It is written, Man shall not live by bread alone, but by every word that proceedeth out of the mouth of God.

Matthew 4:4

This may sound harsh, but if people would spend more time feeding (meditating) their spirits on the Word of God instead of feeding their bodies with food, there would be fewer overweight people (including myself). *Don't fast your spirit, fast your flesh.* Meditation is not difficult. You do it every time you worry. Worry is simply meditating on what Satan tells you. Rather than listening to his words, why not meditate on God's words instead?

Humble yourselves therefore under the mighty hand of God, that he may exalt you in due time: *Casting all your care upon him; for he careth for you.* Be sober, be vigilant; because your adversary the devil, as a roaring lion, walketh about, seeking whom he may devour.

1 Peter 5:6-8

Listen to the words of Jesus as He makes this invitation to you.

> **Come unto me, all ye that labour and are heavy laden, and I will give you rest. Take my yoke upon you, and learn of me; for I am meek and lowly in heart: and ye shall find rest unto your souls. For my yoke is easy, and my burden is light.**
>
> **Matthew 11:28-30**

Meditating on God's Word is essential for good success. We should also commune with God through prayer. Many people don't know how to pray effectively, but Jesus made it quite simple as He demonstrated to His disciples how to pray.

> **Take heed that ye do not your alms before men, to be seen of them: otherwise ye have no reward of your Father which is in heaven.**
>
> **Therefore when thou doest thine alms, do not sound a trumpet before thee, as the hypocrites do in the synagogues and in the streets, that they may have glory of men. Verily I say unto you, They have their reward.**
>
> **But when thou doest alms, let not thy left hand know what thy right hand doeth:**
>
> **That thine alms may be in secret: and thy Father which seeth in secret himself shall reward thee openly.**
>
> **And when thou prayest, thou shalt not be as the hypocrites are: for they love to pray standing in the synagogues and in the corners of the streets, that they may be seen of men. Verily I say unto you, They have their reward.**
>
> **But thou, when thou prayest, enter into thy closet, and when thou hast shut thy door, pray to thy Father which is in secret; and thy Father which seeth in secret shall reward thee openly.**
>
> **But when ye pray, use not vain repetitions, as the heathen do: for they think that they shall be heard for their much speaking.**

Be not ye therefore like unto them: for your Father knoweth what things ye have need of, before ye ask him.

After this manner therefore pray ye: Our Father which art in heaven, Hallowed be thy name.

Thy kingdom come. Thy will be done in earth, as it is in heaven.

Give us this day our daily bread.

And forgive us our debts, as we forgive our debtors.

And lead us not into temptation, but deliver us from evil: For thine is the kingdom, and the power, and the glory, for ever. Amen.

Matthew 6:1-13

Many have learned this prayer word for word but have failed to realize that this is a *model prayer*. It has eight very important steps for us to acknowledge. Let's look at "The Lord's Prayer" again.

After this manner therefore pray ye: Our Father which art in heaven, Hallowed be thy name.

Thy kingdom come. Thy will be done in earth, as it is in heaven.

Give us this day our daily bread.

And forgive us our debts, as we forgive our debtors.

And lead us not into temptation, but deliver us from evil: For thine is the kingdom, and the power, and the glory, for ever. Amen.

Matthew 6:9-13

#1 Our Father which art in heaven. Acknowledge your Heavenly Father. It is He Who is the Provider of all things.

#2 Hallowed be thy name. God is to be revered, praised, worshipped, and honored by His children. (Exodus 20:12, John 4:23–24.)

#3 Thy kingdom come. Thy will be done in earth, as it is in heaven. Pray God's will. His will is His Word. He wants things done on earth as they are in heaven. Is there any disease and sickness in heaven? Is there any poverty in heaven? Is God stealing, killing, and destroying people in heaven? Of course not! This part of the prayer should make it obvious that it is *not* God's will for these things to occur. (John 10:10.) Proclaim His will to be done on earth as it is in heaven and don't listen to the traditional teachings of men.

#4 Give us this day our daily bread. We've now come to the place where it is appropriate to ask God to meet our needs with His provisions. Many people begin their prayer here instead of step #1. Ask in faith according to God's Word and believe that you receive. (See Mark 11:22–24; Matthew 7:7–8, 1 John 5:14–15.)

#5 Forgive us our debts, as we forgive our debtors. Ask God to forgive you in the areas that you have failed. Then forgive others as God has forgiven you. If you don't, the Word of God clearly states your prayers will not be answered. (Matthew 6:14–15, Mark 11:25–26.)

#6 Deliver us from evil. Literally, "deliver us from the evil one." God has given us power over Satan, through the blood of Jesus, by the word of our testimony (Revelation 11:12), and with the whole armor of God. (Ephesians 6:10–18.)

#7 For thine is the kingdom, and the power, and the glory for ever. In God's eternal kingdom we are heirs of God and joint–heirs with Jesus Christ. (Romans 8:16–17.) When Jesus sat down at the right hand of the throne of God He then turned over the power and authority of the kingdom to His church. (Ephesians 1:22.) Read the last chapter of Mark to see what the church has been commissioned to do by the Commander-in-Chief Himself.

#8 Amen. *Amen* is not just a little nicety that we say at the end of a prayer. *Amen* means "so be it," or "it shall be done."(*Strong's Concordance* #281.) *Amen* calls those things

46

that be not as though they were according to the Word of God. (Romans 4:17.) *Amen* is not just a word, it is a word of faith!

Finally, when you pray use this prayer as a model. Yes, it's fine to recite the Lord's prayer word for word, but understand that it is not just a religious prayer. It is an effective method of receiving from the Lord. Your time spent alone in prayer with God will increase your effectiveness when meditating on His Word.

And this is the confidence that we have in him, that, if we ask any thing according to his will, he heareth us:

And if we know that he hear us, whatsoever we ask, we know that we have the petitions that we desired of him.

1 John 5:14-15

If ye abide in me, and my words abide in you, ye shall ask what ye will, and it shall be done unto you.

John 15:7

CHAPTER 4
OBSERVING AND DOING
THE WORD

Now that we can *speak the Word* and *meditate on the Word*, let's look at our next task of *observing* and *doing the Word*. Let's go to God's Word to understand this next condition of success, which is doing God's will.

O that there were such an heart in them, that they would fear me, *and keep all my commandments always,* that it might be well with them, and with their children for ever!

Deuteronomy 5:29

Ye shall observe to do therefore as the Lord your God hath commanded you: ye shall not turn aside to the right hand or to the left.

Ye shall walk in all the ways which the Lord your God hath commanded you, that ye may live, and that it may be well with you, and that ye may prolong your days in the land which ye shall possess.

Deuteronomy 5:32-33

Now these are the commandments, the statutes, and the judgments, which the Lord your God commanded to teach you, *that ye might do them in the land whither ye go to possess it:*

That thou mightest fear the Lord thy God, to keep all his statutes and his commandments, which I command thee, thou, and thy son, and thy son's son, all the days of thy life; and that thy days may be prolonged.

Hear therefore, O Israel, and observe to do it; that it may be well with thee, and that ye may increase mightily, as the Lord God of thy fathers hath promised thee, in the land that floweth with milk and honey.

Deuteronomy 6:1-3

Not every one that saith unto me, Lord, Lord, shall enter into the kingdom of heaven; *but he that doeth the will of my Father which is in heaven.*

Matthew 7:21

Therefore whosoever heareth these sayings of mine, *and doeth them, I will liken him unto a wise man,* which built his house upon a rock.

Matthew 7:24

Teaching them to observe all things whatsoever I have commanded you: and, lo, I am with you alway, even unto the end of the world. Amen.

Matthew 28:20

But he said, Yea rather, *blessed are they that hear the word of God, and keep it.*

Luke 11:28

If ye know these things, *happy are ye if ye do them.*

John 13:17

He that hath my commandments, and keepeth them, he it is that loveth me: and he that loveth me shall be loved of my Father, and I will love him, and will manifest myself to him.

John 14:21

But be ye doers of the word, and not hearers only, deceiving your own selves.

For if any be a hearer of the word, and not a doer, he is like unto a man beholding his natural face in a glass:

For he beholdeth himself, and goeth his way, and straightway forgetteth what manner of man he was.

But whoso looketh into the perfect law of liberty, and continueth therein, he being not a forgetful hearer, *but a doer of the work, this man shall be blessed in his deed.*

James 1:22-25

Blessed are they that do his commandments, that they may have right to the tree of life, and may enter in through the gates into the city.

Revelation 22:14

In addition to these scriptures, the apostle James explains how important it is to mix works along with your faith. (It takes faith to speak and meditate on God's Word.)

Even so faith, if it hath not works, is dead, being alone.

Yea, a man may say, Thou hast faith, and I have works: shew me thy faith without thy works, and I will shew thee my faith by my works.

Thou believest that there is one God; thou doest well: the devils also believe, and tremble.

But wilt thou know, O vain man, that faith without works is dead?

Was not Abraham our father justified by works, when he had offered Isaac his son upon the altar?

Seest thou how faith wrought with his works, and by works was faith made perfect?

And the scripture was fulfilled which saith, Abraham believed God, and it was imputed unto him for righteousness: and he was called the Friend of God.

Ye see then how that by works a man is justified, and not by faith only.

Likewise also was not Rahab the harlot justified by works, when she had received the messengers, and had sent them out another way?

For as the body without the spirit is dead, so faith without works is dead also.

James 2:17-26

See how important it is to *observe and do God's will* along with *speaking and meditating* on the Word? As Joshua 1:8 states, if you combine these commands together, you'll soon be on your way to "good" success, rather than "bad" success. We've all seen many examples of people in the world who have had "bad" success. Money, possessions, power, and influence are not "bad" in and of themselves, but if wrongly used they will bear the fruit of "bad" success. If you are a child of God, however, it is His desire to give you *good things!*

> **Or what man is there of you, whom if his son ask bread, will he give him a stone?**
>
> **Or if he ask a fish, will he give him a serpent?**
>
> **If ye then, being evil, know how to give good gifts unto your children, *how much more shall your Father which is in heaven give good things to them that ask him?***
>
> **Matthew 7:9-11**

Some people who are opposed to prosperity claim money is the root of all evil that corrupts people. But as we learned earlier, that's not true. As the Scripture says:

> **For the *love of money* is the root of all evil: which while some coveted after, they have erred from the faith, and pierced themselves through with many sorrows.**
>
> **But thou, O man of God, flee these things; and follow after righteousness, godliness, faith, love, patience, meekness.**
>
> **Fight the good fight of faith, lay hold on eternal life, whereunto thou art also called, and hast professed a good profession before many witnesses.**
>
> **1 Timothy 6:10-12**

Notice again that Paul says it is the *love of money,* not money itself that is the root of all evil. Don't covet and chase after money. This is a sure way of having "bad" success. In his book, *Things That Are More Important Than Money,* John Avanzini shows from scripture many things that are more important than money, silencing those critics who feel that prosperity teachers distort the truth. Money is a servant of the steward. *The problem is that most people are servants to money, rather than their money serving them.* Why not follow the words of Jesus recorded in the book of Matthew?

No one can serve two masters. Either he will hate the one and love the other, or he will be devoted to the one and despise the other. *You cannot serve both God and Money.*

Therefore I tell you, do not worry about your life, what you will eat or drink; or about your body, what you will wear. Is not life more important than food, and the body more important than clothes?

Look at the birds of the air; they do not sow or reap or store away in barns, and yet your heavenly Father feeds them. Are you not much more valuable than they?

Who of you by worrying can add a single hour to his life?

And why do you worry about clothes? See how the lilies of the field grow. They do not labor or spin.

Yet I tell you that not even Solomon in all his splendor was dressed like one of these.

If that is how God clothes the grass of the field, which is here today and tomorrow is thrown into the fire, will he not much more clothe you, O you of little faith?

So do not worry, saying, "What shall we eat?" or "What shall we drink?" or "What shall we wear?"

For the pagans run after all these things, and your heavenly Father knows that you need them.

But seek first his kingdom and his righteousness, and all these things will be given to you as well.

Matthew 6:24-33 (NIV)

After accepting Jesus Christ as my Lord and Saviour and then a few months later receiving the baptism of the Holy Spirit, I prayed and dedicated my life according to Matthew 6:33. I then began to tithe. Immediately God began fulfilling His promise of "adding these things unto me." Within one year, I was married. Not only did God give me a beautiful Christian woman (whom I met in church) , but I also received a father-in-law, mother-in-law, sister-in-law, and brother-in-law at the same time. While engaged, I introduced my best friend, Jerry, to my future sister-in-law Tammy. He started coming to church with me and turned his life over to Jesus too. Jerry and Tammy were married exactly 11 months to the day after Regina and I were married.

Before our first year anniversary, my wife and I moved from a rented condominium into our very own home. God then moved us to Church of the Harvest where my Pastor preaches and teaches the uncompromising Word of God. By the end of our second year of marriage my business was doing so well that my wife could quit her job (my income had quadrupled since I began tithing two years prior). We were then able to buy a bigger, newly built home. My second business is booming and I'm about to start a third. On June 21, 1994 we had a baby girl, Taylor Ashleigh. Our friends and family keep growing. Other blessings are just too numerous to mention. *I have truly been blessed by God and give Him all the glory!*

The only credit that I can take is that I listened to the *voice of the Holy Spirit* as He showed me that the *Word of God was true.* I applied His Word to my life and it worked (and is still working). Since God is no respecter of persons, what He has done for me and so many others, He'll do for you. Just live according to His Word.

How can a young man keep his way pure? By living according to your word.

I seek you with all my heart; do not let me stray from your commands.

I have hidden your word in my heart that I might not sin against you.

Praise be to you, O Lord; *teach me your decrees.*

With my lips I recount all the laws that come from your mouth.

I rejoice in following your statutes as one rejoices in great riches.

I meditate on your precepts and consider your ways.

I delight in your decrees; I will not neglect your word.

Psalm 119:9-16 (NIV)

The person who has the "good success" of Joshua 1:8 delights in God's decrees and does not neglect His Word.

Kenneth Copeland's father once said that if he ever discovered that God wasn't real, that Jesus didn't die on the cross, the Holy Spirit didn't come to earth, and the Word of God wasn't true, *he would still continue living the same way because the Word was working in his life!*

I couldn't agree more!!

But the truth is, *God is real! Jesus died on the cross, was buried, rose again, and is now seated at the right hand of Almighty God. The Holy Spirit did in fact come to earth (and He's still here), and that's why the Word works!*

CHAPTER 5
GOD'S WORDS
VERSUS MAN'S WORDS

Throughout this book, you may be wondering why there are so many scriptures compared to the amount of the author's words. The reason is very simple. Man's words and traditions are worth *nothing* when compared to the inspired words of God.

It is the Word of God that makes the difference in people's lives. As Paul states in Romans:

> *Yea, let God be true, but every man a liar;* **as it is written, That thou mightest be justified in thy sayings, and mightest overcome when thou art judged.**
>
> **Romans 3:4**

And listen to the very own words of Jesus, as He spoke to the religious leaders of His day, the Pharisees, as recorded by Matthew and Mark:

> *Thus have ye made the commandment of God of none effect by your tradition.*
>
> **Ye hypocrites, well did Esaias prophesy of you, saying,**
>
> **This people draweth nigh unto me with their mouth, and honoureth me with their lips; but their heart is far from me.**
>
> **But in vain they do worship me, teaching for doctrines the commandments of men.**
>
> **Matthew 15:6-9**

Making the word of God of none effect through your tradition, which ye have delivered: and many such like things do ye.

Mark 7:13

Many churches are still making the Word of God of none effect because of denominational traditions and religious doctrines. This is one reason why "church" has left a bad taste in the mouths of many people. However, there are great churches that believe, preach, and teach the inspired Word of God from Genesis to Revelation. These churches have taken a stand to believe and trust God's Word instead of the words, opinions, and traditions of man. Where does your church stand on this issue?

The middle verse of the Bible makes this statement:

It is better to trust in the Lord than to put confidence in man.

Psalm 118:8

Some people have a problem with the divine inspiration of the Bible. It seems somewhat ironic to me that God chose Psalm 118:8 to be the middle verse of the Bible.

In his book, *Hidden Prophecies in the Psalms*, J. R. Church makes this very interesting observation. "The 118th Psalm is located between the shortest chapter (Psalm 117) and the longest chapter (Psalm 119) in the Bible and it contains the middle verse. There are 1,188 chapters in the Christian Bible, 594 chapters before and 594 chapters after Psalm 118:8. It is remarkable to note that 594 plus 594 make a sum total of 1188—which is the number of the chapter and verse which contains the middle verse."

"It must be more than a coincidence. Yet the design could not have been made by the psalmist who compiled this portion of the Psalms centuries before the New Testament was written, or by the others who organized the order of the books. The Old Testament was compiled in its accepted form hundreds of years before the New Testament was compiled in its accepted order. The Geneva Bible, printed in the sixteenth century, was the first Bible to be printed with verse divisions. By then, it was too late to arrange the books in such an order as to make Psalms 117–119 fit into the center of the Scriptures. By that time they were already there. Only divine design could have ordered this phenomenon."

The Bible is the inspired Word of God. The Bible teaches that every word was inspired by the Holy Spirit, written through men. This is called "Plenary *Verbal* Inspiration" of Scripture. The Prophets, Jewish Rabbis and early church historians all held this view. However, modern scholarship during the last few centuries has embraced another view called "Plenary *Dynamic* Inspiration," which means that man played a much greater role in composing and compiling the books of the Bible. These scholars (and many denominations) believe that most of the books of the Bible were not written by the original authors. They also attempt to minimize the significance of the prophetic scriptures concerning Jesus and the last days. They label the hundreds of instances in the Bible that point to divine design as mere coincidences.

One such "coincidence" we just mentioned is at the heart of God's Word in Psalm 118:8. It is the eternal message to trust and place your confidence in Him and only Him. "Good success" will be obtained when men and women realize that God's Words (the Bible) should be placed far above man's words, thoughts, and traditions. Now, some religious teachers still claim that we can't be sure of the Word of God since it was written by men. However, instead of debating these scholars, let's see what the Bible says on this issue.

As he spake by the mouth of his holy prophets, which have been since the world began.

Luke 1:70

We have also a more sure word of prophecy; whereunto ye do well that ye take heed, as unto a light

that shineth in a dark place, until the day dawn, and the day star arise in your hearts:

Knowing this first, that no prophecy of the scripture is of any private interpretation.

For the prophecy came not in old time by the will of man: *but holy men of God spake as they were moved by the Holy Ghost.*

2 Peter 1:19-21

All scripture is given by inspiration of God, and is profitable for doctrine, for reproof, for correction, for instruction in righteousness:

That the man of God may be perfect, thoroughly furnished unto all good works.

2 Timothy 3:16-17

First Corinthians also shows us that God's Word did not come about by man's words or opinions but by the Holy Spirit.

But God hath revealed them unto us by his Spirit: for the Spirit searcheth all things, yea, the deep things of God.

For what man knoweth the things of a man, save the spirit of man which is in him? Even so the things of God knoweth no man, but the Spirit of God.

Now we have received, not the spirit of the world, but the spirit which is of God; that we might know the things that are freely given to us of God.

Which things also we speak, not in the words which man's wisdom teacheth, but which the Holy Ghost teacheth; comparing spiritual things with spiritual.

But the natural man receiveth not the things of the Spirit of God: for they are foolishness unto him: neither can he know them, because they are spiritually discerned.

But he that is spiritual judgeth all things, yet he himself is judged of no man.

For who hath known the mind of the Lord, that he may instruct him? But we have the mind of Christ.

1 Corinthians 2:10-16

How do we distinguish between the traditions of men from the words of Almighty God? It's simple. *By using the Word of God!* The traditions of men are usually formulated in the *soulish* realm which is the mind and intellect. Just as God is Triune, so is man a triune being.

And the very God of peace sanctify you wholly; and I pray God your whole *spirit and soul and body* be preserved blameless unto the coming of our Lord Jesus Christ.

1 Thessalonians 5:23

You are a *spirit* that has a *soul* and you live in a *body*.

The Greek word for *soul* in this passage is *psuche.* (*Strong's Concordance* #5590.) This is where we get our word *psyche* which means *the mind.*

If you could see your spirit man separated from your body, what would he look like? Would he look strong and healthy, or would he be a puny little thing because he hasn't had any Word to eat? We know how possible it is to eat too much physical food and become overweight. It is equally possible to have so much intellectual (soulish) knowledge that one's head becomes too big to walk through the doorway.

However, your spirit man can never become overweight or bigheaded because of an overfeeding of the Word. He can only grow stronger and stronger. If you are having problems with your body, (health, weight, etc.) or problems with your mind (bad thoughts, desires, pride, etc.) it is most likely because you haven't been feeding your spirit man. Determine to make a change today and get into God's Word. *Feed your spirit with His Spirit.* The Word of God is spirit food that can be used to make the distinction between the things of God and the intellectual ideas of man.

For the word of God is living and powerful, and sharper than any two-edged sword, *piercing even to the division of soul and spirit,* and of joints and marrow,

and is a discerner of the thoughts and intents of the heart.

Hebrews 4:12 (NKJV)

Successful Christians have learned once they elevate the Word of God to its proper place, their life of defeat and mediocrity is radically changed into a life of victory and triumph. Believe God! Believe His Word! Unlike man, He does not lie nor does He change His mind!

He who is the Glory of Israel *does not lie or change his mind*; for he is not a man, that he should change his mind.

1 Samuel 15:29 (NIV)

Jesus Christ *the same yesterday, and to day, and for ever.*

Hebrews 13:8

It is up to each individual to spend quality time in God's Word. To be truly successful in life, we must become dedicated students of Scripture, willing to dig deep to discover what He has for each of us.

Study to shew thyself approved unto God, a workman that needeth not to be ashamed, *rightly dividing the word of truth.*

2 Timothy 2:15

TIP #6

This is sometimes difficult, but to achieve greater success in life you must put away, forget, and bury all ideas, concepts, beliefs, and traditions that are contrary to God's Word, especially when it comes to finances. Many teachers try to downplay the significance of the Economic Laws that are found in Scripture. However, consider this: Of the 1,188 chapters of the Bible, there are more than 1,500 verses relating to finances (on the average more than one scripture per chapter). Of the 38 parables of Jesus, 16 of them have to do with finances. Obviously, finances are very important in the kingdom of God.

Who do you place your trust in and obey? God or man?

> **Then Peter and the other apostles answered and said, We ought to obey God rather than men.**
>
> **Acts 5:29**

For continued success in life, let's turn to the book of Proverbs.

> *Trust in the Lord with all thine heart;* **and lean not unto thine own understanding.**
>
> *In all thy ways acknowledge him, and he shall direct thy paths.*
>
> **Be not wise in thine own eyes: fear the Lord, and depart from evil.**
>
> *It shall be health to thy navel, and marrow to thy bones.*
>
> **Honour the Lord with thy substance, and with the firstfruits of all thine increase** (tithing):
>
> **So shall thy barns be filled with plenty, and thy presses shall burst out with new wine.**
>
> **Proverbs 3:5-10**

When you were in your mother's womb, all life-sustaining nourishment came through the umbilical cord. The scar of your navel (or as we say in Oklahoma, your "belly button") should be a constant reminder of that. God's Word feeds your spirit in much the same way. Likewise, a person in need of a bone marrow transplant knows how important marrow is to the body. Without marrow, life can only be sustained for a short period of time. This again is true of God's Word.

TIP #7

The book of Proverbs contains 31 chapters of the wisdom of God. You can receive the wisdom of these 31 chapters if you'll start your day reading with the chapter that corresponds to the date. For example, if today is the 16th of the month, start by reading Proverbs 16 before you start the class. Then tomorrow

---

TIP #7 cont.
read chapter 17, and so on. Do this each month, month
after month. You'll be amazed with the results. Also
read the "Wisdom Psalms" regularly which are Psalms
1, 36, 37, 49, 72, 73, 112, 119, 127, 128, and 133.
Incidentally, the book of Proverbs contains 234 verses
about wealth and prosperity, the most of any book
found in the Bible.

To illustrate the importance of believing God's Word
instead of man's, let's review a story of someone you have
studied in history. Unfortunately, history books have
deleted most of the details you will learn here.

In 1492, only Christopher Columbus (who was a
Christian) and a few others held the idea that the earth
was round. Today it seems silly but in that day *almost
everyone in the world believed that the earth was flat!* They also
thought that Columbus was a fool for having such wild
beliefs.

Had you and I been alive in that era, what do you think
we would have believed? Was the earth really flat or was it
round? Difficult question. Not really if we were acquainted
with God's Word as Columbus was.

> **Have ye not known? have ye not heard? hath it not
> been told you from the beginning? have ye not
> understood from the foundations of the earth?**
> *It is he that sitteth upon the circle of the earth,* **and
> the inhabitants thereof are as grasshoppers; that
> stretcheth out the heavens as a curtain, and spreadeth
> them out as a tent to dwell in:**
> **That bringeth the princes to nothing; he maketh the
> judges of the earth as vanity.**
>
> Isaiah 40:21-23

Isaiah the prophet wrote this passage somewhere
between 740 and 680 years *before* Jesus Christ was born.
Approximately 1,492 years *after* Jesus' birth, when Columbus
set sail, the common belief was that the world was flat. Those

who dared to challenge this "world belief" were ridiculed and labeled as fools. However, this great scientific truth was in God's Word all the time. Then along came Columbus, a Christian, and very knowledgeable about the Scriptures. He dared to use his faith and disregarded the prevalent belief of this world's system and changed the world. Isn't it interesting how most of us learned as children that Columbus was a hero, but in this last decade the media has painted quite a different picture of him.

Although Columbus did not find the alternate trading route he was seeking, he was nevertheless right in the final analysis and made one of the greatest discoveries of all time. The New World! This New World became a "Promised Land" to millions of people for many centuries.

Think for a moment about grace, mercy, meekness, forgiveness of sin, salvation, baptism, healing, the Holy Spirit, prayer, faith, victory, communion, abundance, prosperity, and success. All of these things are found in God's Word, yet what is the basis for your beliefs on these topics, man's traditions, or God's Word? First Corinthians 2:5 says that your faith should not be in the wisdom of men, but in the power of God!

One of my favorite scriptures of the entire Bible fits this chapter perfectly. It just sends chills down the spine of those who support the religious teachings of man. Memorize it. You'll need it often to combat the religious zealots and traditional teachings of man!

> God forbid: yea, *let God be true, but every man a liar;* as it is written, That thou mightest be justified in thy sayings, and mightest overcome when thou art judged.
>
> **Romans 3:4**

Let the basis for your decisions on doctrinal issues be based on God's Word and not on man's teachings and traditions.

During my life I have learned many things were not taught to me correctly. After getting into God's Word, I learned to believe and trust in Him. Once you've done that, you will easily discern when someone is trying to teach you their own opinion rather than expounding on what God's Word really says.

In the stock and commodity markets, small traders and brokers are typically wrong 85 percent of the time in their trading decisions. If you and everyone else you know are positioned on the same side of the market, it's a good sign that you will be on the losing side of the trade. Likewise, wisdom shows that it makes sense to do some searching before going along too quickly with the crowd.

> **Enter ye in at the strait gate:** *for wide is the gate, and broad is the way, that leadeth to destruction, and many there be which go in thereat:*
>
> **Because strait is the gate, and narrow is the way, which leadeth unto life, and few there be that find it.**
> **Matthew 7:13-14**
>
> **All this have I proved by wisdom: I said, I will be wise; but it was far from me.**
>
> **That which is far off, and exceeding deep, who can find it out?**
>
> *I applied mine heart to know, and to search, and to seek out wisdom, and the reason of things, and to know the wickedness of folly, even of foolishness and madness:*
> **Ecclesiastes 7:23-25**

Wisdom is critical if you are going to understand the things of God.

> *For the preaching of the cross is to them that perish foolishness; but unto us which are saved it is the power of God.*
>
> **For it is written, I will destroy the wisdom of the wise, and will bring to nothing the understanding of the prudent.**

Where is the wise? where is the scribe? where is the disputer of this world? *Hath not God made foolish the wisdom of this world?*

For after that in the wisdom of God the world by wisdom knew not God, it pleased God by the foolishness of preaching to save them that believe.

For the Jews require a sign, and the Greeks seek after wisdom:

But we preach Christ crucified, unto the Jews a stumblingblock, and unto the Greeks foolishness;

But unto them which are called, both Jews and Greeks, Christ the power of God, and the wisdom of God.

Because the foolishness of God is wiser than men; and the weakness of God is stronger than men.

For ye see your calling, brethren, how that not many wise men after the flesh, not many mighty, not many noble, are called:

But God hath chosen the foolish things of the world to confound the wise; and God hath chosen the weak things of the world to confound the things which are mighty;

And base things of the world, and things which are despised, hath God chosen, yea, and things which are not, to bring to nought things that are:

That no flesh should glory in his presence.

But of him are ye in Christ Jesus, who of God is made unto us wisdom, and righteousness, and sanctification, and redemption:

That, according as it is written, He that glorieth, let him glory in the Lord.
                                     1 Corinthians 1:18-31

The proverbs of Solomon the son of David, king of Israel;

To know wisdom and instruction; to perceive the words of understanding;

To receive the instruction of wisdom, justice, and judgment, and equity;

To give subtilty to the simple, to the young man knowledge and discretion.

A wise man will hear, and will increase learning; and a man of understanding shall attain unto wise counsels:

To understand a proverb, and the interpretation; the words of the wise, and their dark sayings.

The fear of the Lord is the beginning of knowledge: but fools despise wisdom and instruction.

Proverbs 1:1-7

The "Fear (reverence/worship) of the Lord" is the beginning of wisdom. If you have been trying it "man's way" all your life and have been unsuccessful, you may want to listen to Proverbs 14:12:

There is a way which seemeth right unto a man, but the end thereof are the ways of death.

Why not choose "God's Way" and follow His Word instead of man's? If you do, one day this scripture will be said of your life.

So mightily grew the word of God and prevailed.

Acts 19:20

CHAPTER 6
HAVE YOU READ GOD'S LAST WILL AND TESTAMENT?

God's Word is His Last Will and Testament to you! Your success is based on what you know about *who you are, your rights, your privileges, and your inheritance.* If you don't know about your *will,* how can you know what's rightfully yours?

What you don't know can hurt you!

Suppose for a moment you were a son or daughter of a very wealthy man who died. You were then given a document to read that listed all your rights and privileges, in addition to a detailed plan how to obtain your inheritance. What would you do? Would you read the will or would you use the document to decorate your coffee table or bookshelf?

It's safe to say, without hesitation *you would read the will!*

How much more shall the blood of Christ, who through the eternal Spirit offered himself without spot to God, purge your conscience from dead works to serve the living God?

***And for this cause he is the mediator of the new testament, that by means of death,* for the redemption of the transgressions that were under the first testament, they which are called might receive the promise of eternal inheritance.**

For where a testament is, there must also of necessity be the death of the testator.

Hebrews 9:14-16

Jesus Christ signed that very "Testament" (God's Word) with His own blood when He was crucified on Calvary some 2,000 years ago. Jesus is the "Mediator" or "Executor" of the New Testament. The words "Testament," "Mediator," and "Executor," are legal words. In fact, some translations of the Bible call the New Testament, "The Last Will and Testament of Jesus Christ." It is truly a legal document.

Let's look again at Hebrews 9:16-17:

> **For where a testament is, there must also of necessity be the death of the testator.**
>
> *For a testament is of force after men are dead:* **otherwise it is of no strength at all while the testator liveth.**

In God's Word you will discover how Jesus' *death,* burial, and resurrection, has provided an inheritance for you. Yes, the Bible talks frequently about your inheritance. Are you interested in receiving it?

> **And now, brethren, I commend you to God, and to the word of his grace, which is able to build you up, and to give you an *inheritance* among all them which are sanctified.**
>
> **Acts 20:32**
>
> **To open their eyes, and to turn them from darkness to light, and from the power of Satan unto God, that they may receive forgiveness of sins, and *inheritance* among them which are sanctified by faith that is in me.**
>
> **Acts 26:18**
>
> **In whom also we have obtained an *inheritance,* being predestinated according to the purpose of him who worketh all things after the counsel of his own will.**
>
> **Ephesians 1:11**
>
> **Which is the earnest of our *inheritance* (the Holy Spirit) until the redemption of the purchased possession, unto the praise of his glory.**
>
> **Ephesians 1:14**

The eyes of your understanding being enlightened; that ye may know what is the hope of his calling, and what the riches of the glory of his *inheritance* in the saints.

Ephesians 1:18

For this ye know, that no whoremonger, nor unclean person, nor covetous man, who is an idolater, hath any *inheritance* in the kingdom of Christ and of God.

Ephesians 5:5

Giving thanks unto the Father, which hath made us meet to be partakers of the *inheritance* of the saints in light.

Colossians 1:12

Knowing that of the Lord ye shall receive the reward of the *inheritance:* for ye serve the Lord Christ.

Colossians 3:24

The Spirit itself beareth witness with our spirit, that we are the children of God:

And if children, then heirs; heirs of God, and joint-heirs with Christ.

Romans 8:16-17

And from Jesus Christ, who is the faithful witness, and the first begotten of the dead, and the prince of the kings of the earth. Unto him that loved us, and washed us from our sins in his own blood,

And hath made us kings and priests unto God and his Father; to him be glory and dominion for ever and ever.

Revelation 1:5-6

Because God wanted to make the unchanging nature of his purpose very clear to *the heirs of what was promised,* he confirmed it with an oath.

God did this so that, by two unchangeable things in which it is impossible for God to lie, we who have fled to take hold of the hope offered to us may be greatly encouraged.

71

We have this hope as an anchor for the soul, firm and secure. It enters the inner sanctuary behind the curtain,

Where Jesus, who went before us, has entered on our behalf. He has become a high priest forever, in the order of Melchizedek.

Hebrews 6:17-20 (NIV)

Born–again believers can obtain their inheritance by *speaking God's Word, meditating on His Word,* and by *observing and doing His Word.* (Remember Joshua 1:8.) However, your inheritance is not for you to "squander," but to be a blessing to others.

As the apostle James states:

Ye ask, and receive not, because ye ask amiss, *that ye may consume it upon your lusts.*

James 4:3

But as God prophesied to Abraham in the book of Genesis:

And I will make of thee a great nation, and I will bless thee, and make thy name great; and thou shalt be a blessing:

And I will bless them that bless thee, and curse him that curseth thee: and in thee shall all families of the earth be blessed.

Genesis 12:2-3

It is quite difficult to be a blessing if you are not blessed yourself. Abraham was blessed of God. He was the father of the Jews as well as the "father of faith" to Christians. Reread verse three again.

And I will bless them that bless thee, and curse him that curseth thee: and in thee shall all families of the earth be blessed.

This should be a warning to those who think it profitable to curse Jews and Christians in this day. God looks out for His people.

You've learned in this chapter that your inheritance is found in God's Word. His Word is *truth*. His Word is *faith*. His Word is *prosperity*. His Word is *success*. Do you believe His Word?

> So shall my word be that goeth forth out of my mouth: it shall not return unto me void, but it shall accomplish that which I please, *and it shall prosper in the thing whereto I sent it.*
>
> **Isaiah 55:11**

> But as it is written, Eye hath not seen, nor ear heard, neither have entered into the heart of man, the things which God hath prepared for them that love him.
>
> *But God hath revealed them unto us by his Spirit:* for the Spirit searcheth all things, yea, the deep things of God.
>
> For what man knoweth the things of a man, save the spirit of man which is in him? Even so the things of God knoweth no man, but the Spirit of God.
>
> Now we have received, not the spirit of the world, but the spirit which is of God; that we might know the things that are freely given to us of God.
>
> Which things also we speak, not in the words which man's wisdom teacheth, but which the Holy Ghost teacheth; comparing spiritual things with spiritual.
>
> But the natural man receiveth not the things of the Spirit of God: for they are foolishness unto him: neither can he know them, because they are spiritually discerned.
>
> But he that is spiritual judgeth all things, yet he himself is judged of no man.
>
> For who hath known the mind of the Lord, that he may instruct him? *But we have the mind of Christ.*
>
> **1 Corinthians 2:9-16**

Jesus Christ is the only testator who has ever died, then come back to life for the specific purpose of guaranteeing that His will, word, and testament would remain in effect to all who would believe in Him and call upon His Name. *No one else has ever done this.* Menu of the Hindu's did not (1100's B.C.), the Chinese man Confucius did not (1100's B.C.), Gotama Budda did not (600's B.C.), and Mohammed, founder of Islam (the newest religion in the world), did not (600's A.D). *Only Jesus Christ, the Son of the Living God, died and rose again, conquering death, hell, and the grave!*

Some Christians do not like the idea of people studying the religions of the world. I couldn't disagree more! When you closely analyze the false religions, you will quickly see how they are so similar to one another, yet entirely opposed to Christianity. You will learn many interesting things when you take time to study the religions of the world. Many of them borrow and pervert stories and doctrines found in the Bible, while other religions invent new ways that man can approach God.

Even in Christianity we find man's traditions about approaching God are often not based on scripture. However, God speaks very clear on this doctrinal issue too.

> (God) **who will have all men to be saved, and to come unto the knowledge of the truth. For there is one God,** *and one mediator between God and men, the man Christ Jesus;* **Who gave himself a ransom for all, to be testified in due time.**
>
> 1 Timothy 2:4-6

God wishes all to be saved and come to the knowledge of the truth. What a glorious inheritance we have in the Last Will and Testament of Jesus Christ!

CHAPTER 7
TRUE SUCCESS BEGINS HERE!

For the preaching of the cross is to them that perish foolishness; but unto us which are saved it is the power of God.

1 Corinthians 1:18

The promise of true prosperity and success mentioned in Joshua 1:8 is conditioned on *speaking the Word, meditating on the Word,* and *doing God's Word.* However, a person who is yet to believe on the name of the Lord Jesus Christ cannot carry out the above three actions.

It is interesting to note that the name *Joshua* and the name *Jesus* come from the same Hebrew name *Yeshua.* Just as Joshua led his people into the promised land under the Old Covenant, Jesus will lead His people into the promised land under the New Covenant.

But what saith it? The word is nigh thee, even in thy mouth, and in thy heart: that is, the word of faith, which we preach;

That if thou shalt confess with thy mouth the Lord Jesus, and shalt believe in thine heart that God hath raised him from the dead, thou shalt be saved.

For with the heart man believeth unto righteousness; and with the mouth confession is made unto salvation.

For the scripture saith, Whosoever believeth on him shall not be ashamed.

For there is no difference between the Jew and the Greek: for the same Lord over all is rich unto all that call upon him.

For whosoever shall call upon the name of the Lord shall be saved.

How then shall they call on him in whom they have not believed? and how shall they believe in him of whom they have not heard? and how shall they hear without a preacher?

And how shall they preach, except they be sent? as it is written, How beautiful are the feet of them that preach the gospel of peace, and bring glad tidings of good things!

But they have not all obeyed the gospel. For Esaias (Isaiah) saith, Lord, who hath believed our report?

So then faith cometh by hearing, and hearing by the word of God.

Romans 10:8-17

It takes *faith* to believe on the name of Jesus Christ. This is the absolute starting point for every believer. Unfortunately, most people and their denominations believe this is where everything stops too. As it takes *faith* to receive Jesus Christ as your personal Savior, it also takes *faith* to receive the Holy Spirit Who was promised by Jesus both before and after His death on the cross.

But the Comforter, which is the Holy Ghost, whom the Father will send in my name, he shall teach you all things, and bring all things to your remembrance, whatsoever I have said unto you.

John 14:26

And he said unto them, These are the words which I spake unto you, while I was yet with you, that all things must be fulfilled, which were written in the law of Moses, and in the prophets, and in the psalms, concerning me.

Then opened he their understanding, that they might understand the scriptures.

And said unto them, Thus it is written, and thus it behoved Christ to suffer, and to rise from the dead the third day:

And that repentance and remission of sins should be preached in his name among all nations, beginning at Jerusalem.

And ye are witnesses of these things.

And, behold, I send the promise of my Father upon you: but tarry ye in the city of Jerusalem, until ye be endued with power from on high.

And he led them out as far as to Bethany, and he lifted up his hands, and blessed them.

And it came to pass, while he blessed them, he was parted from them, and carried up into heaven.

And they worshipped him, and returned to Jerusalem with great joy:

And were continually in the temple, praising and blessing God. Amen.

Luke 24:44-53

In the above scripture, **until ye be endued with** *power* **from on high**, refers to the Holy Spirit. This will be even more evident in the next few scriptures, but let's look up this word *power* in the Greek.

The word *power* is translated *dunamis* in the Greek. This is where we get our English word *dynamo*. *Strong's Concordance* #1411 defines *dunamis (doo'-nam-is)* as: "*a force (literally or figuratively); specially, miraculous power (usually by implication, a miracle itself):* KJV— *ability, abundance, meaning, might (-ily, -y, -y deed), (worker of) miracle (-s), power, strength, violence, mighty (wonderful) work.*"

The Holy Spirit is the *dynamo* or the *power* available to those believers who have accepted Jesus Christ. But He (like Jesus) will not force Himself on those who do not have the faith to believe what the scriptures say about Him. Each and every person who has believed that the Father (the First Person of the Trinity) sent His only Begotten Son, Jesus, (the Second Person of the Trinity) has also been given the Holy Spirit (the Third Person of the Trinity).

However, many believers have yet to release the power of the Holy Spirit that resides in them. This release comes through the baptism of the Holy Spirit. Although salvation is still intact, they will never realize their full potential of success if they continue discounting the *power* of the Holy Spirit.

Don't settle for a watered-down, powerless gospel just because that's the way you were taught by man's traditions. Instead, believe God's Word. As it is written, the Holy Spirit was there "in the beginning."

In the beginning God created the heaven and the earth.

And the earth was without form, and void; and darkness was upon the face of the deep. *And the Spirit of God moved upon the face of the waters.*

Genesis 1:1-2

Let's look further to see what the Word of God says about the Holy Spirit, His power, and the manifestation of His presence.

And he said unto them, Go ye into all the world, and preach the gospel to every creature.

He that believeth and is baptized shall be saved; but he that believeth not shall be damned.

And these signs shall follow them that believe; In my name shall they cast out devils; *they shall speak with new tongues;*

They shall take up serpents; and if they drink any deadly thing, it shall not hurt them; *they shall lay hands on the sick,* **and they shall recover.**

So then after the Lord had spoken unto them, he was received up into heaven, and sat on the right hand of God.

And they went forth, and preached every where, the Lord working with them, and confirming the word with signs following. Amen.

Mark 16:15-20

Until the day in which he was taken up, after that he through the Holy Ghost had given commandments unto the apostles whom he had chosen:

To whom also he shewed himself alive after his passion by many infallible proofs, being seen of them forty days, and speaking of the things pertaining to the kingdom of God:

And, being assembled together with them, commanded them that they should not depart from Jerusalem, *but wait for the promise of the Father,* which, saith he, ye have heard of me.

For John truly baptized with water; but ye shall be baptized with the Holy Ghost not many days hence.

Acts 1:2-5

As always, after the promise comes the *manifestation.*

And when the day of Pentecost was fully come, they were all with one accord in one place.

And suddenly there came a sound from heaven as of a rushing mighty wind, and it filled all the house where they were sitting.

And there appeared unto them cloven tongues like as of fire, and it sat upon each of them.

And they were all filled with the Holy Ghost, and began to speak with other tongues, as the Spirit gave them utterance.

Acts 2:1-4

Later in the book of Acts, we find Paul talking about the Holy Ghost.

He said unto them, Have ye received the Holy Ghost since ye believed? And they said unto him, We have not so much as heard whether there be any Holy Ghost.

And he said unto them, Unto what then were ye baptized? And they said, Unto John's baptism.

Then said Paul, *John verily baptized with the baptism of repentance,* saying unto the people, that they

should believe on him which should come after him,
that is, on Christ Jesus.

When they heard this, they were baptized in the
name of the Lord Jesus.

And when Paul had laid his hands upon them, the
Holy Ghost came on them; and they spake with
tongues, and prophesied.

Acts 19:2-6

Every believer should ask himself the same question as
in verse 2. "Have you received the Holy Spirit since you've
believed?"

Later in Paul's ministry, he spoke the following to the
Corinthians:

I thank my God, *I speak with tongues* more than ye
all...

Wherefore, brethren, covet to prophesy, *and forbid
not to speak with tongues.*

1 Corinthians 14: 18, 39

The evidence of the infilling, or baptism of the Holy
Spirit (speaking in tongues), was also prophesied by Isaiah
in the Old Testament.

Whom shall he teach knowledge? and whom shall
he make to understand doctrine? them that are weaned
from the milk, and drawn from the breasts.

For precept must be upon precept, precept upon
precept; line upon line, line upon line; here a little, and
there a little:

*For with stammering lips and another tongue will he
speak to this people.*

Isaiah 28:9-11

Paul also tells us in Romans that by praying in the
Spirit, our spirit makes intercession for us according to the
will of God.

Likewise the Spirit also helpeth our infirmities: for
we know not what we should pray for as we ought: but

the Spirit itself maketh intercession for us with groanings which cannot be uttered.

And he that searcheth the hearts knoweth what is the mind of the Spirit, *because he maketh intercession for the saints according to the will of God.*

Romans 8:26-27

The Holy Spirit prays through our spirit if we will allow Him. When you don't know what to pray for, pray in the Holy Spirit. Praying in the Spirit will always be according to the will of God. Please realize that the Holy Spirit was given to every believer as a deposit until Jesus returns with His raptured church for the millennial reign. This is recorded in the first chapter of Ephesians.

Blessed be the God and Father of our Lord Jesus Christ, who hath blessed us with all spiritual blessings in heavenly places in Christ:

According as he hath chosen us in him before the foundation of the world, that we should be holy and without blame before him in love:

Having predestinated us unto the adoption of children by Jesus Christ to himself, according to the good pleasure of his will,

To the praise of the glory of his grace, wherein he hath made us accepted in the beloved.

In whom we have redemption through his blood, the forgiveness of sins, according to the riches of his grace;

Wherein he hath abounded toward us in all wisdom and prudence;

Having made known unto us the mystery of his will, according to his good pleasure which he hath purposed in himself:

That in the dispensation of the fullness of times he might gather together in one all things in Christ, both which are in heaven, and which are on earth; even in him:

In whom also we have obtained an inheritance, being predestinated according to the purpose of him who worketh all things after the counsel of his own will:

That we should be to the praise of his glory, who first trusted in Christ.

In whom ye also trusted, after that ye heard the word of truth, the gospel of your salvation: in whom also after that ye believed, ye were sealed with that Holy Spirit of promise,

Which is the earnest of our inheritance until the redemption of the purchased possession, unto the praise of his glory.

Wherefore I also, after I heard of your faith in the Lord Jesus, and love unto all the saints,

Cease not to give thanks for you, making mention of you in my prayers;

That the God of our Lord Jesus Christ, the Father of glory, may give unto you the spirit of wisdom and revelation in the knowledge of him:

The eyes of your understanding being enlightened; that ye may know what is the hope of his calling, and what the riches of the glory of his inheritance in the saints,

And what is the exceeding greatness of his power to us-ward who believe, according to the working of his mighty power,

Which he wrought in Christ, when he raised him from the dead, and set him at his own right hand in the heavenly places,

Far above all principality, and power, and might, and dominion, and every name that is named, not only in this world, but also in that which is to come:

And hath put all things under his feet, and gave him to be the head over all things to the church,

Which is his body, the fulness of him that filleth all in all.

Ephesians 1:3-23

In the italicized words, *earnest of our inheritance,* the word *earnest* has the following descriptions in *Strong's Concordance*:

New Testament Greek—*728: arrhabon (ar-hrab-ohn'); of Hebrew origin [6162]; a pledge, i.e. part of the purchase-money or property given in advance as security for the rest. KJV— earnest.*

Old Testament Hebrew–*6162: 'arabown (ar-aw-bone'); from 6148 (in the sense of exchange); pawn (given as security): KJV— pledge.*

The Holy Spirit is this deposit, earnest, pledge, and inheritance that God has given to each born-again believer who will receive Him. To illustrate, most everyone knows how important *deposits* are in a bank account. If you've ever sold a house, you know that the *earnest money* (also called *good faith* money) is given to you as a security that the contract will be fulfilled. Also, lenders know how important it is for collateral to be *pledged* before a loan can be given. Finally, those who have received an abundant inheritance from a deceased family member can attest to the significance of a *will and testament.* The Holy Spirit is this power, the dynamo that supercharges believers and causes them to do great exploits, exceeding what they could ever dream or imagine.

Now unto him that is able to do exceeding abundantly above all that we ask or think, according to the power that worketh in us.

Ephesians 3:20

But as it is written, Eye hath not seen, nor ear heard, neither have entered into the heart of man, the things which God hath prepared for them that love him.

***But God hath revealed them unto us by his Spirit:* for the Spirit searcheth all things, yea, the deep things of God.**

For what man knoweth the things of a man, save the spirit of man which is in him? even so the things of God knoweth no man, but the Spirit of God.

Now we have received, not the spirit of the world, but the spirit which is of God; that we might know the things that are freely given to us of God.

Which things also we speak, not in the words which man's wisdom teacheth, but which the Holy Ghost teacheth; comparing spiritual things with spiritual.

But the natural man receiveth not the things of the Spirit of God: for they are foolishness unto him: neither can he know them, because they are spiritually discerned.

But he that is spiritual judgeth all things, yet he himself is judged of no man.

For who hath known the mind of the Lord, that he may instruct him? *But we have the mind of Christ.*

1 Corinthians 2:9-16

For there are three that bear record in heaven, the Father, the Word, and the Holy Ghost: and these three are one.

1 John 5:7

Initial success begins after believing God's Word and accepting Jesus Christ. Success continues and then becomes supercharged and powered by the Holy Spirit into the life of the believer.

Who can receive Jesus Christ and the Holy Spirit? Everyone who asks and calls on His name! God is no respecter of persons.

Then Peter opened his mouth, and said, Of a truth I perceive that God is no respecter of persons.

Acts 10:34

Some people think they have to get their life cleaned up *before* they can get right with God. Others may feel that they have committed too many sins or were involved in such gross sin that God would never forgive them. Nothing could be further from the truth. All you have to do is confess your sin and you will be forgiven. Where there is great sin, you'll find even greater grace for forgiveness of sin.

But not as the trespass, so also (is) the free gift. For if by the trespass of the one the many died, much more did the grace of God, and the gift by the grace of the one man, Jesus Christ, abound unto the many.

And not as through one that sinned, (so) is the gift: for the judgment (came) of one unto condemnation, but the free gift (came) of many trespasses unto justification.

For if, by the trespass of the one, death reigned through the one; much more shall they that receive the abundance of grace and of the gift of righteousness reign in life through the one, (even) Jesus Christ.

So then as through one trespass (the judgment came) unto all men to condemnation; even so through one act of righteousness (the free gift came) unto all men to justification of life.

For as through the one man's disobedience the many were made sinners, even so through the obedience of the one shall the many be made righteous.

And the law came in besides, that the trespass might abound; *but where sin abounded, grace did abound more exceedingly:*

That, as sin reigned in death, even so might grace reign through righteousness unto eternal life through Jesus Christ our Lord.

Romans 5:15-21 (ASV)

For all have sinned, and come short of the glory of God.

Romans 3:23

If we say that we have fellowship with him, and walk in darkness, we lie, and do not the truth:

But if we walk in the light, as he is in the light, we have fellowship one with another, and the blood of Jesus Christ his Son cleanseth us from all sin.

If we say that we have no sin, we deceive ourselves, and the truth is not in us.

If we confess our sins, he is faithful and just to forgive us our sins, and to cleanse us from all unrighteousness.

**If we say that we have not sinned, we make him a
liar, and his word is not in us.**

1 John 1:6-10

The word *righteousness* sounds like a difficult concept
for most people to grasp. On the contrary it is quite simple.
Righteousness means "right standing with God." However,
some people think since they have participated in some
Christian ritual—were submerged or sprinkled with water,
or because they attend church on Easter or Christmas—
they are right with God. First John 2:3-6 shows how you can
tell if you are walking with, or running from God.

**And hereby we do know that we know him, if we
keep his commandments.**

**He that saith, I know him, and keepeth not his
commandments, is a liar, and the truth is not in him.**

**But whoso keepeth his word, in him verily is the
love of God perfected: hereby know we that we are in
him.**

**He that saith he abideth in him ought himself also
so to walk, even as he walked.**

1 John 2:3-6

*Each Person of the Trinity is there to guarantee the success of
the believer.* Be ready for the final outpouring of the Holy
Spirit upon all believers who'll receive Him in these last of
the last days as promised by the prophet Joel.

**And it shall come to pass afterward, that I will pour
out my spirit upon all flesh; and your sons and your
daughters shall prophesy, your old men shall dream
dreams, your young men shall see visions:**

**And also upon the servants and upon the
handmaids in those days will I pour out my spirit.**

**And I will shew wonders in the heavens and in the
earth, blood, and fire, and pillars of smoke.**

**The sun shall be turned into darkness, and the
moon into blood, before the great and the terrible day
of the Lord come.**

And it shall come to pass, that whosoever shall call on the name of the Lord shall be delivered: for in mount Zion and in Jerusalem shall be deliverance, as the Lord hath said, and in the remnant whom the Lord shall call.

Joel 2:28-32

Peter alluded to this when the Holy Spirit came upon believers at Pentecost, the birthday of the church.

And they were all amazed, and were in doubt, saying one to another, What meaneth this?

Others mocking said, These men are full of new wine.

But Peter, standing up with the eleven, lifted up his voice, and said unto them, Ye men of Judaea, and all ye that dwell at Jerusalem, be this known unto you, and hearken to my words:

For these are not drunken, as ye suppose, seeing it is but the third hour of the day.

But this is that which was spoken by the prophet Joel;

And it shall come to pass in the last days, saith God, I will pour out of my Spirit upon all flesh: and your sons and your daughters shall prophesy, and your young men shall see visions, and your old men shall dream dreams:

And on my servants and on my handmaidens I will pour out in those days of my Spirit; and they shall prophesy:

And I will shew wonders in heaven above, and signs in the earth beneath; blood, and fire, and vapour of smoke:

The sun shall be turned into darkness, and the moon into blood, before that great and notable day of the Lord come:

And it shall come to pass, that whosoever shall call on the name of the Lord shall be saved.

Acts 2:9,13

This signified the beginning of the last days according to God's timetable. Since this happened almost 2,000 years ago, it seems apparent that we are now living in the last of the last days.

At the turn of this century starting in California and Kansas, a revival not seen since the day of Pentecost began to sweep across the nation (and the world), affecting every denomination of the body of Christ. At the same time as this final outpouring and manifestation of God's Spirit upon believers, there is another movement occurring in the world during these last days. Paul writes to Timothy about this other outpouring.

This know also, *that in the last days perilous times shall come.*

For men shall be lovers of their own selves, covetous, boasters, proud, blasphemers, disobedient to parents, unthankful, unholy,

Without natural affection, trucebreakers, false accusers, incontinent, fierce, despisers of those that are good,

Traitors, heady, highminded, lovers of pleasures more than lovers of God;

Having a form of godliness, but denying the power thereof: **from such turn away.**

For of this sort are they which creep into houses, and lead captive silly women laden with sins, led away with divers lusts,

Ever learning, and never able to come to the knowledge of the truth.

Now as Jannes and Jambres withstood Moses, so do these also resist the truth: men of corrupt minds, reprobate concerning the faith.

But they shall proceed no further: for their folly shall be manifest unto all men, as theirs also was.

But evil men and seducers shall wax worse and worse, deceiving, and being deceived.

2 Timothy 3:1-9,13

Does this not accurately describe the attitude of our society?

During these last days we are seeing the wicked becoming increasingly more wicked. In June of 1962, during the Kennedy administration, prayer was removed from school classrooms and then the Bible. Staggering increases in murder, robbery, rape, child abuse, abortion, alcoholism, drug use, fatal diseases, teen pregnancy, and suicide began to occur after this Supreme Court decision. Coincidence? Hardly!

We have seen the Clinton administration support and sponsor taxpayer-funded abortions, as well as gays in the Armed Forces. The government felt that prayer and Bible reading would corrupt our children, but there are politicians and government leaders who endorse the distribution of condoms and the teaching of homosexuality as an alternate lifestyle to our children in the classroom. Instead of policing the schools for bubble gum and spit wad offenders, we now have metal detectors to check for weapons. Haven't our schools come a long way since 1962? However, despite the decay of our society, there is still hope!

> **Righteousness exalteth a nation: but sin is a reproach to any people.**
>
> **Proverbs 14:34**

> **Blessed is the nation whose God is the Lord; and the people whom he hath chosen for his own inheritance.**
>
> **The Lord looketh from heaven; he beholdeth all the sons of men.**
>
> **From the place of his habitation he looketh upon all the inhabitants of the earth.**
>
> **Psalm 33:12-14**

> **If my people, which are called by my name, shall humble themselves, and pray, and seek my face, and**

turn from their wicked ways; then will I hear from heaven, and will forgive their sin, and will heal their land.

2 Chronicles 7:14

TIP #8

Every person should check the voting record of all public office holders and candidates. You may be quite surprised to learn the voting record of many elected officials differs from their campaign rhetoric. The Christian Coalition publishes a scorecard that shows the voting record of your congressmen as well as other pertinent information about candidates who are seeking office. Vote for candidates whose track records are in line with God's Word instead of worrying about which party they belong to.

These final outpourings of light and darkness are happening concurrently. The number of people caught in the middle is disappearing. Everyone must make a choice, God or Satan, Christ or antichrist, Holy Spirit or false prophet, life or death, wheat or tares, sheep or goats, light or darkness, hot or cold, victory or defeat, saved or lost. Which side do you choose?

CHAPTER 8
HAVING THE "GOD KIND OF FAITH"

But what saith it? The word is nigh thee, even in thy mouth, and in thy heart: that is, *the word of faith,* which we preach;

So then *faith cometh by hearing,* and *hearing by the word of God.*

Romans 10:8,17

We know that faith comes from the Word of God, but what exactly is faith? Man has many opinions, but let's turn again to the Word for the answer. For God's definition of faith, open your Bible to the eleventh chapter of Hebrews. This is known as the great "faith chapter" of the Bible. As Jerry Savelle says, "Those mentioned in Hebrews 11 are the 'heritage' or 'ancestors' of our faith. God's definition of faith is found in the first three verses of this great chapter.

Now faith is the substance of things hoped for, the evidence of things not seen.

For by it the elders obtained a good report.

Through faith we understand that the worlds were framed by the word of God, so that things which are seen were not made of things which do appear.

Hebrews 11:1-3

Faith is an invisible substance. *The Amplified Bible* states that *faith* is "*the assurance, the confirmation, the title deed of the things we hope for.*" Now, the world thinks that *hope* means "to wish." However, Kenneth Copeland points out that the Word of God teaches that *hope* is "*the intensive, earnest expectation that what God has promised will come to pass."* Jesus expounds on the power of faith in the gospel of Mark.

> And Jesus answering saith unto them, *Have faith in God.*
>
> For verily I say unto you, That whosoever shall say unto this mountain, Be thou removed, and be thou cast into the sea; and shall not doubt in his heart, but shall believe that those things which he saith shall come to pass; he shall have whatsoever he saith.
>
> Therefore I say unto you, *What things soever ye desire, when ye pray, believe that ye receive them, and ye shall have them.*
>
> Mark 11:22-24

The italicized words of the first sentence, *Have faith in God*, literally mean "have the faith of God" or have the "God kind of faith." Finnis Jennings Dake, Bible scholar of this century stated: *"This faith is possible or it would not be a command."* Man was created with God's faith but doubt entered in at the fall. (Genesis 3:1–7.) Faith is restored in the new birth and if normally exercised and maintained it will grow to fullness and power. For further study see Romans 1:5, 17; 10:17; Galatians 2:20; Colossians 1:23; 2:6–7; 2 Thessalonians 1:3; 2 Peter 1:5.

Doubt, fear, and unbelief (which entered in at the fall) are the exact opposites of faith. Unsuccessful people, whether knowingly or unknowingly, follow Satan when they operate in doubt, fear, and unbelief (reverse faith) just as Adam and Eve did. Why not follow Jesus, the Word of God, and expect miracles to happen in your life. Or, would you rather let doubt, fear, and unbelief rob you of God's miraculous power and His many precious promises?

> And when he was come into his own country, he taught them in their synagogue, insomuch that they were astonished, and said, Whence hath this man this wisdom, and these mighty works?

> Is not this the carpenter's son? is not his mother called Mary? and his brethren, James, and Joses, and Simon, and Judas?
>
> And his sisters, are they not all with us? Whence then hath this man all these things?
>
> And they were offended in him. But Jesus said unto them, A prophet is not without honour, save in his own country, and in his own house.
>
> And he did not many mighty works there because of their unbelief.
>
> **Matthew 13:54-58**

Don't let unbelief hinder the mighty works that Jesus wants to do in your life. Scripture records that Jesus only marveled at two things while on earth, people's faith and people's lack of faith. Jesus commands us to exercise our faith through prayer and petitions (as well as asking for the Holy Spirit). We just learned in the last chapter that God is not a respecter of persons, *but he is a respecter of faith!* Without faith it is impossible to please God!

> *But without faith it is impossible to please him:* **for he that cometh to God must believe that he is, and that he is a rewarder of them that diligently seek him.**
>
> **Hebrews 11:6**

Abraham was called righteous because of his faith.

> *Therefore it is of faith, that it might be by grace; to the end the promise might be sure to all the seed; not to that only which is of the law, but to that also which is of the faith of Abraham;* who is the father of us all,
>
> (As it is written, I have made thee a father of many nations,) before him whom he believed, even God, who quickeneth the dead, and calleth those things which be not as though they were.
>
> *Who against hope believed in hope, that he might become the father of many nations,* according to that which was spoken, So shall thy seed be.

And being not weak in faith, he considered not his own body now dead, when he was about an hundred years old, neither yet the deadness of Sarah's womb:

He staggered not at the promise of God through unbelief; but was strong in faith, giving glory to God;

And being fully persuaded that, what he had promised, he was able also to perform.

And therefore it was imputed to him for righteousness.

Romans 4:16-22

Read verse 17 again. ... **and calleth those things which be not as though they were.** And verse 18, **Who against hope believed in hope.** And in verse 20, **He staggered not at the promise of God through unbelief; but was strong in faith, giving glory to God.** This is the type of faith that God expects us to have. Once we make the decision to walk by faith as Abraham did, we too will have the victory that overcomes the world.

For whatsoever is born of God overcometh the world: and this is the victory that overcometh the world, even our faith.

Who is he that overcometh the world, but he that believeth that Jesus is the Son of God?

1 John 5:4-5

The foundation of this faith is built upon accepting of Jesus as your Lord and Saviour, then receiving the baptism (release) of the Holy Spirit. Your faith will then be strengthened by spending time in the Word, through praying with your understanding, and by praying in the Spirit.

But you, beloved, building yourselves up on your most holy faith, *praying in the Holy Spirit.*

Jude 20 (NKJV)

The effectual fervent prayer of a righteous man availeth much.

James 5:16

> And I say unto you, *Ask,* and it shall be given you; *seek,* and ye shall find; *knock,* and it shall be opened unto you.
>
> For every one that asketh receiveth; and he that seeketh findeth; and to him that knocketh it shall be opened.
>
> If a son shall ask bread of any of you that is a father, will he give him a stone? or if he ask a fish, will he for a fish give him a serpent?
>
> Or if he shall ask an egg, will he offer him a scorpion?
>
> If ye then, being evil, know how to give good gifts unto your children: how much more shall your heavenly Father give the Holy Spirit to them that ask him?
>
> **Luke 11:9-13**

Ask! And you will receive. *Seek!* And you will find. *Knock!* And it shall be opened (businessmen involved in sales should have this scripture memorized). Sounds simple, yet few people have enough faith to try God's Word to see if it works. Others ask for the wrong reasons.

> **From whence come wars and fightings among you? come they not hence, even of your lusts that war in your members?**
>
> **Ye lust, and have not: ye kill, and desire to have, and cannot obtain: ye fight and war, *yet ye have not, because ye ask not.***
>
> *Ye ask, and receive not, because ye ask amiss, that ye may consume it upon your lusts.*
>
> **James 4:1-3**

But you might ask, "What are the conditions for believers to receive what they ask for or to have what they say?" There are only two.

Condition #1 is that *the Father must be glorified in the Son.* This is found in the gospel of John. Notice the part the Holy Spirit plays.

Believe me that I am in the Father, and the Father in me: or else believe me for the very works' sake.

Verily, verily, I say unto you, He that believeth on me, the works that I do shall he do also; and greater works than these shall he do; because I go unto my Father.

And whatsoever ye shall ask in my name, that will I do, *that the Father may be glorified in the Son.*

If ye shall ask any thing in my name, I will do it.

If ye love me, keep my commandments.

And I will pray the Father, and he shall *give you another Comforter,* that he may abide with you for ever;

Even the Spirit of truth; whom the world cannot receive, because it seeth him not, neither knoweth him: but ye know him; for he dwelleth with you, and shall be in you.

John 14:11-17

Condition # 2 is found in 1 John. *We must ask according to His Will (His Word).*

These things have I written unto you that believe on the name of the Son of God; that ye may know that ye have eternal life, and that ye may believe on the name of the Son of God.

And this is the confidence that we have in him, that, *if we ask any thing according to his will, he heareth us:*

And if we know that he hear us, whatsoever we ask, we know that we have the petitions that we desired of him.

1 John 5:13-15

Asking according to God's Will is the same as asking according to His Word. *God's Will is His Word. His Word is His Will.* In a previous chapter we learned about the Word being God's Last Will and Testament. It is the same principle here. The Bible is God's Testament, Will, and Covenant to all who'll receive.

If you are unsure what God's Word says, isn't it time you found out?

TIP #9

Spend several days studying the book of Hebrews, especially chapters 10, 11, and 12. Look up the stories of each person listed in chapter 11 and discover why they were noted for their "great faith." Faith can work for you just like it did for these people of the Bible who are your "spiritual ancestors." Jerry Savelle has some great messages on this topic. Order some tapes from his ministry. His address is at the back of this book.

Faith is extremely important! Never, ever, let anyone take away your faith! When you decide to put God's Word first and believe in His promises, there will be many people waiting in line (family, friends, co-workers, even some clergymen) to tell you that it (faith) won't work for you. You'll hear the labels "name it and claim it" or "grab it and bag it" attached to those who preach the Word of Faith. But whatever is said, don't let go of your faith. Listen to what God has promised you in His Word. *Speak it, meditate on it, and do it!*

> Let us hold fast *the profession of our faith* without wavering; for he is faithful that promised.
>
> **Hebrews 10:23**

The *New King James Version* says it a little differently.

> Let us hold fast *the confession of our hope* without wavering, for He who promised is faithful.

The *King James Version* says "the profession of our faith", while the *New King James Version* translates it more clearly "the confession of our hope." This *hope* is the anchor of the soul.

> *This hope we have as an anchor of the soul,* both sure and steadfast, and which enters the Presence behind the veil.
>
> **Hebrews 6:19 (NKJV)**

Let's look at Hebrews 10:23 from *The Amplified Bible*.

So let us seize and hold fast and retain without wavering the hope we cherish and confess and our acknowledgement of it, for He Who promised is reliable (sure) and faithful to His word.

Profess your faith by confessing your hope but don't doubt or waver. James shows us how costly that can be.

But let him ask in faith, nothing wavering. For he that wavereth is like a wave of the sea driven with the wind and tossed.

For let not that man think that he shall receive any thing of the Lord.

A double minded man is unstable in all his ways.
James 1:6-8

Don't let doubt creep into your faith. Rather, receive from God's Word and you'll see that He truly has a divine prosperity plan prepared just for you.

He that spared not his own Son, but delivered him up for us all, how shall he not with him also *freely give us all things?*
Romans 8:32

According as his divine power hath given unto us all things that pertain unto life and godliness, through the knowledge of him that hath called us to glory and virtue:

Whereby are given unto us exceeding great and precious promises: that by these ye might be partakers of the divine nature, having escaped the corruption that is in the world through lust.
2 Peter 1:3-4

"For I know the plans I have for you," declares the Lord, "plans to prosper you and not to harm you, plans to give you hope and a future.

"Then you will call upon me and come and pray to me, and I will listen to you.

"You will seek me and find me when you seek me with all your heart.

"I will be found by you," declares the Lord.

Jeremiah 29:11-14 (NIV)

This chapter has demonstrated the importance of having the "God kind of faith" operating in our lives as a powerful *offensive* weapon. However, in Paul's letter to the Ephesians, we find that the "shield of faith" is listed as one of our spiritual *defensive* weapons too.

Finally, my brethren, be strong in the Lord, and in the power of his might.

Put on the whole armour of God, that ye may be able to stand against the wiles of the devil.

For we wrestle not against flesh and blood, but against principalities, against powers, against the rulers of the darkness of this world, against spiritual wickedness in high places.

Wherefore take unto you the whole armour of God, that ye may be able to withstand in the evil day, and having done all, to stand.

Stand therefore, having your loins girt about with truth, and having on the breastplate of righteousness;

And your feet shod with the preparation of the gospel of peace;

Above all, taking the shield of faith, wherewith ye shall be able to quench all the fiery darts of the wicked.

And take the helmet of salvation, and the sword of the Spirit, which is the word of God:

Praying always with all prayer and supplication in the Spirit, and watching thereunto with all perseverance and supplication for all saints.

Ephesians 6:10-18

In football, it takes a great offense *and* a great defense to have a truly successful team. *So it is with your faith!*

Let's look at these weapons of our warfare again.

> *Wherefore take unto you the whole armour of God,* that ye may be able to withstand in the evil day, and having done all, to stand.
>
> Stand therefore, *having your loins girt about with truth,* and having on the breastplate of righteousness;
>
> And *your feet shod with the preparation of the gospel of peace;*
>
> Above all, *taking the shield of faith,* wherewith ye shall be able to quench all the fiery darts of the wicked.
>
> *And take the helmet of salvation,* and the *sword of the Spirit,* which is the word of God:
>
> *Praying always with all prayer and supplication in the Spirit,* and watching thereunto with all perseverance and supplication for all saints.
>
> **Ephesians 6:13-18**

Many Christians choose to do battle without the complete armor of God. Later they wonder why they haven't been victorious to the extent that the Word has promised them. To this day, many denominations are still running around wearing nothing but their "helmets of salvation." Imagine how funny that looks in the spirit realm to be running around with nothing on but a helmet.

As I was going to print with this book, I began to come across the path of individuals who opposed the faith and prosperity message (they need to read chapter 5). In fairness to them I've listed some of the common criticisms of the "faith message."

— "Faith teachers are obnoxious and preach that if something bad is happening in your life, you are in sin."

— "The message of faith tells people that they can make God give them things they want regardless of the condition of their heart."

— "Faith preachers tell people it is God's Will for them to be healed. Then people have false hope and backslide when they're not healed."

— "The faith message tells people that they should become like God, speaking, declaring, and making things come to pass."

Critics of the faith message should go to their *Strong's Concordance* and look up how many verses contain the words "faith" and "prosperity." Then each individual scripture containing those words should be thoroughly analyzed. (It should take a great deal of time to accomplish this task.)

Finally, Hebrews 11:6 should be reviewed again and again:

> **But without faith it is impossible to please Him: for he that cometh to God must believe that he is, and that he is a rewarder of them that diligently seek him.**

Now, about the issue of people abusing the "faith message."

— Our government misleads the public on many occasions, but I still vote in each election and continue to pay my taxes.

— Electricity kills hundreds of people each year, but I still use it to cook my food, heat and cool my home, and to watch my television.

— Automobile accidents claim the lives of thousands every year, yet I drive my automobile to work each day.

— People jump off tall buildings and commit suicide, but I still go in and out of tall buildings all the time.

— Guns are used by drug dealers to kill people, yet I still use my gun to go dove and quail hunting.

— Money is sometimes duplicated by counterfeiters, yet I still keep using my money to purchase the things I need and want.

— People take God's Scripture and pervert it, yet I continue to read, meditate, and speak the Word of God every day.

Just because someone attempts to pervert the "faith message," don't let that rob you of your faith in God's Word. Listen to Paul's words again from the book of Romans.

> **For what if some did not believe? shall their unbelief make the faith of God without effect?**
>
> **God forbid: yea, let God be true, but every man a liar; as it is written, That thou mightest be justified in thy sayings, and mightest overcome when thou art judged.**
>
> **Romans 3:3-4**

Still others make the claim that faith isn't that important based on 1 Corinthians 13:1–3:

> **Though I speak with the tongues of men and of angels, and have not charity, I am become as sounding brass, or a tinkling cymbal.**
>
> **And though I have the gift of prophecy, and understand all mysteries, and all knowledge; and though I have all faith, so that I could remove mountains, and have not charity, I am nothing.**
>
> **And though I bestow all my goods to feed the poor, and though I give my body to be burned, and have not charity, it profiteth me nothing.**

Love is of course the most important thing of all. God is love. However, Paul never intended for people to abandon faith because of love. First Corinthians 13 demonstrates that love should be the motivator of tongues, prophecy, faith, and giving to the poor. If you are not motivated by God's love, the above can still take place, but it will bear no fruit for you afterwards.

Without love, *tongues* can still take place.

Without love, *prophecy* can still take place.

Without love, *faith* can still move mountains.

Without love, *giving to the poor* can still take place.

All of the above can take place without love, but your works will *profit you nothing if they're not done in love!* However, this does not mean that faith is the stepchild of love. Rather, love should always be the *motivater* of faith.

Remember, God's Word does not say, "Without *love* it is impossible to please Him." No, the Bible says:

But without faith it is impossible to please him: for he that cometh to God must believe that he is, and that he is a rewarder of them that diligently seek him.
Hebrews 11:6

Nor does it say, "*Love* cometh by hearing and hearing by the Word of God." No, it says:

So then faith cometh by hearing, and hearing by the word of God.
Romans 10:17

It is by *faith* that you receive Jesus as Lord and Saviour. It is by *faith* that you receive the Holy Spirit. Likewise it is by *faith* that you can receive healing for your body and prosperity for your household. *Every aspect of the Word of God works only by faith!* This "faith message" is God's Word, not man's word. As the apostle Paul states in Romans (which is a quote from Deuteronomy):

But what saith it? The word is nigh thee, even in thy mouth, and in thy heart: that is, the word of faith, which we preach.
Romans 10:8

Faith is not the stepchild of love. Rather, faith and love are brothers working together to reveal the fullness of God.

That Christ may dwell in your hearts by faith; that ye, being rooted and grounded in love, **may be able to comprehend with all saints what is the breadth, and** length, and depth, and height; and to know the love of Christ, which passeth knowledge, that ye might be filled with all the fulness of God.

Ephesians 3:17-19

CHAPTER 9
THE ANOINTED ONE
AND HIS ANOINTING

And it shall come to pass in that day, that his burden shall be taken away from off thy shoulder, and his yoke from off thy neck, and the yoke shall be destroyed because of the *anointing*.
Isaiah 10:27

In about 700 B.C., the prophet Isaiah prophesied under the influence of the Holy Spirit that there would be a "day" that burdens would be taken off the shoulders of people and yokes would be removed, completely destroyed by the "anointing." Later in his ministry, Isaiah made another interesting prophecy.

The Spirit of the Lord God is upon me; because the Lord hath *anointed* me to preach good tidings unto the meek; he hath sent me to bind up the brokenhearted, to proclaim liberty to the captives, and the opening of the prison to them that are bound.
Isaiah 61:1

Jesus quoted this very scripture on the first day of His public ministry.

And there was delivered unto him the book of the prophet Esaias (Isaiah). And when he had opened the book, he found the place where it was written,
The Spirit of the Lord is upon me, because he hath *anointed* me to preach the gospel to the poor; he hath sent me to heal the brokenhearted, to preach deliverance to the captives, and recovering of sight to the blind, to set at liberty them that are bruised,

To preach the acceptable year of the Lord.

And he closed the book, and he gave it again to the minister, and sat down. And the eyes of all them that were in the synagogue were fastened on him.

And he began to say unto them, This day is this scripture fulfilled in your ears.

Luke 4:17-21

Let's look closely at the Hebrew and Greek words and their meanings which contain the root word *anoint.*

According to *Strong's Concordance,* the Hebrew word for *anointing* in Isaiah 10:27 is *shemen* which means:

8081 shemen (sheh'-men); from 8080; grease, especially liquid (as from the olive, often perfumed); figuratively, richness: KJV— anointing, fat (things), fruitful, oil ([-ed]), ointment, olive, + pine.

In Isaiah 61:1, the Hebrew word for *anointed* is *mashach:*

4886 mashach (maw-shakh'); a primitive root; to rub with oil, i.e. to anoint; by implication, to consecrate; also to paint: KJV— anoint, paint.

This is where we get the term "Messiah" which is translated as "His Anointed" as found in Psalm 2:2.

Why do the heathen rage, and the people imagine a vain thing?

The kings of the earth set themselves, and the rulers take counsel together, against the Lord, and against *his anointed.*

Psalm 2:1-2

His Anointed is translated and defined by *Strong's* as:

4899 mashiyach (maw-shee'-akh);from 4886; anointed; usually a consecrated person (as a king, priest, or saint); specifically, the Messiah: KJV— anointed, Messiah.

Jewish people for centuries had awaited their Messiah, the Anointed One, Who would free them from bondage and deliver them from their oppressors. Christians of course recognize this "Messiah" as the person of Jesus Christ. In fact, the Greek word for *Christ* is a translation of the Hebrew word *Messiah*. Contrary to popular belief, *Christ* is not Jesus' last name. He is Jesus, "The Messiah," or Jesus, "The Anointed One and His anointing."

The word *Christ* is used over 300 times in the New Testament. Let's look at this Greek word from *Strong's Concordance*.

5547 Christos (khris-tos'); from 5548; anointed, i.e. the Messiah, an epithet of Jesus: KJV— Christ.

Notice how the word *Christ* #5547 is taken from #5548 which means "anointed." This word is used in Acts 10:38.

How God *anointed* Jesus of Nazareth with the Holy Ghost and with power: who went about doing good, and healing all that were oppressed of the devil; for God was with him. **Acts 10:38**

Looking once again at Strong's, this word *anointed* is defined as:

5548 chrio (khree'-o); probably akin to 5530 through the idea of contact; to smear or rub with oil, i.e. (by implication) to consecrate to an office or religious service: KJV— anoint.

Everytime you read the word *Christ* in the New Testament, think about who and what you are really reading about. Your focus should be on "The Anointed One and His anointing." Jesus came to tell people they no longer had to be poor, sick, or separated from God. His purpose was to destroy the works of the devil (1 John 3:8) and to restore our relationship to God (Hebrews 9). That's the good news of the gospel! Now, we Christians are responsible for proclaming this message in the same manner as Jesus. (Mark 16:15–18.) *Christians?* If we are going to call ourselves *Christians*, shouldn't we have a better understanding of this word too?

5546 Christianos (khris-tee-an-os'); from 5547; a Christian, i.e. follower of Christ: KJV— Christian.

Christians or *followers of Christ* could also be translated "the followers of the Anointed One and His anointing" or simply "Anointeds." Acts 11:26 states that the disciples were first called Christians, or Anointeds, at Antioch. Are you one of the *Anointeds?* Do you have an *anointing* on your life like those in the book of Acts? Do you walk around with the Anointed One and His anointing on the inside of you? Let's look also at the Greek word for *anointing*.

5545 chrisma (khris'-mah); from 5548; an unguent or smearing, i.e. (figuratively) the special endowment ("chrism") of the Holy Spirit: KJV— anointing, unction.

This is where we get our English word *charisma*, but its true meaning is a *special endowment* from the Holy Spirit. "Charismatic" churches believe and operate in the gifts and anointings of the Holy Spirit.

Since we've looked at quite a few Hebrew and Greek words with the root *anoint*, let's summarize them.

STRONG'S	ENGLISH	HEB/GRK	MEANING
8081	anointing	*shemen*	to grease with liquid
4886	anointed	*mashach*	to rub with oil
4899	His Anointed	*mashiyach*	The Messiah
5548	anointed	*chrio*	to smear, rub with oil
5547	Christ	*Christos*	Anointed One, His Anointing
5546	Christians	*Christianos*	followers of the Anointed One
5545	anointing	*chrisma*	unction, special endowment

After hearing Kenneth Copeland preach on the *Anointing* at the Southwest Believers' Convention in Fort Worth, Texas, I began this indepth word study on "The Anointed One and His anointing." My initial reaction to the message was indifferent since I thought I already knew that the word *Christ* meant *Messiah*. However, I soon discovered that the anointing was a subject that was much more vast than I had suspected. Every time I saw the word *Christ* in the New Testament, I would replace it with "The Anointed One and His anointing" and meditate on it. For example:

> **To whom God would make known what is the riches of the glory of this mystery among the Gentiles; which is** *Christ (The Anointed One and His Anointing)* **in you, the hope of glory, whom we preach.**
> **Colossians 1:27-28**

Doesn't that shed a little more light on who and what is in you? Let's look at another scripture from Philipians.

> **I can do all things through** *Christ (The Anointed One and His Anointing)* **which strengtheneth me.**
> **Philippians 4:13**

It is the Anointed One and His anointing inside of us that enables us to do all things. However, just as there is the *anointing,* there is the *antianointing.*

> **For many deceivers are entered into the world, who confess not that Jesus Christ is come in the flesh. This is a deceiver and** *an antichrist (against the Anointed One and His anointing).*
> **2 John 1:7**

> **Little children, it is the last time: and as ye have heard that** *antichrist* **shall come, even now are there many** *antichrists (anti or against the anointing);* **whereby we know that it is the last time.**
> **1 John 2:18**

Those who deny Jesus as the Messiah or "Anointed One" are called "antichrists" in this scripture. Most of us have heard about the Antichrist, the satanically inspired leader who will appear at the end of the age. However, the spirt of antichrist is not just upon those who reject Jesus, The Anointed One, but the spirit of antichrist is also upon those who reject the message of His anointing.

Most people in the body of Christ do not reject Jesus as the Messiah, but how often do we hear of denominations and individuals who reject His Anointing to heal, to bless, and to restore all that the enemy has stolen. We learned earlier that Isaiah 10:27 says the anointing *removes burdens and destroys yokes.* Since these *yokes* (sickness, poverty, and separation from God) are listed in Isaiah 61:1, let's look at this Scripture again.

> **The Spirit of the Lord God is upon Me, because the Lord has anointed Me to preach good tidings to the poor; He has sent Me *to heal* the brokenhearted, *to proclaim liberty* to the captives, and *the opening of the prison* to those who are bound;**
> **To proclaim the acceptable year of the Lord....**
> **Isaiah 61:1-2**

The Anointed One came *to heal, to proclaim liberty, and to open prison.* We already know about healing but what about *proclaiming liberty* and *opening prison?* To *proclaim liberty* goes along with the next verse which speaks of *the acceptable year of the Lord.* This is a reference to the Year of Jubilee as found in Leviticus 25:10, which provides for all debts to be cancelled and lost possessions to be restored. *The opening of prison,* according to *Strong's Concordance,* actually means *salvation from sin..* Healing, liberty, and freedom are all accomplished by the anointing.

Remember Jesus stated in Luke 4:16–22 that He was the fulfillment of the prophecy of Isaiah. Jesus was anointed to heal you, to prosper you, and to restore you to a right relationship with God. His purpose was to redeem mankind from the *curse of the law. The curse* is found in Deuteronomy 28:15–68 while *the blessing* is found in Deuteronomy 28:1–14.

> *Christ (The Anointed One and His anointing)* **hath redeemed us from the curse of the law,** being made a curse for us: for it is written, Cursed is every one that hangeth on a tree:
>
> **That the blessing of Abraham might come on the Gentiles through Jesus Christ; that we might receive the promise of the Spirit through faith.**
>
> Galatians 3:13-14

Jesus and His anointing have redeemed us from the curse of the law. However, most people have a hard time believing that. You'll hear people teach that God is the One Who brings sickness, disease, and poverty upon people to teach them lessons and keep them humble. Others are suspicious of people who prosper. This is the spirit of antichrist or the "anti-anointing" at its fullest. Not one time in the New Testament do you ever find Jesus proclaiming that God is the author of sickness, disease, and poverty while Satan is the one handing out all the blessings. But we do find Jesus saying and doing exactly the opposite throughout the New Testament.

> **The thief cometh not, but for to steal, and to kill, and to destroy: I am come that they might have life, and that they might have it more abundantly.**
>
> John 10:10

> **How God anointed Jesus of Nazareth with the Holy Ghost and with power: who went about doing good, and healing all that were oppressed of the devil; for God was with him.**
>
> Acts 10:38

> **He that committeth sin is of the devil; for the devil sinneth from the beginning. For this purpose the Son of God was manifested, that he might destroy the works of the devil.**
>
> 1 John 3:8

This same anointing that was on Jesus is promised to everyone in the body of Christ.

> For the Son of God, Jesus Christ, who was preached
> among you by us— by me, Silvanus, and Timothy—
> was not Yes and No, but in Him was Yes. For all the
> promises of God in Him are Yes, and in Him Amen, to
> the glory of God through us. Now He who establishes
> us with you in Christ and has *anointed* us is God, *who*
> *also has sealed us and given us the Spirit in our hearts as*
> *a guarantee.*
> **2 Corinthians 1:19-22 (NKJV)**

Just as God *anointed* Jesus, He will also *anoint* His
children by giving them the Holy Spirit. It is this *anointing*
that enables us to do all things through Christ, *the Anointed*
One. It is by the *anointing* that we lay hands on the sick and
they recover. It is by the *anointing* that we speak to the
mountains and they are cast into the sea. It is by the
anointing that we continue to pray for our loved ones until
they come into the kingdom. It is by the *anointing* that God
gives us the power to get wealth. It is the *anointing* that
removes burdens and destroys yokes. *This anointing*
empowers us to live the life of faith.

I've noticed that those who discount what the Bible
says about healing and prosperity are usually against the
"faith message" too. They fail to realize that it takes the
same faith to receive salvation as it does to receive healing
for your body and abundance in your life. Grace works
through faith.

> Even when we were dead in sins, hath quickened
> us together with Christ, (by grace ye are saved;)
>
> And hath raised us up together, and made us sit
> together in heavenly places in Christ Jesus:
>
> That in the ages to come he might shew the
> exceeding riches of his grace in his kindness toward us
> through Christ Jesus.
>
> *For by grace are ye saved through faith;* and that not
> of yourselves: it is the gift of God:
>
> Not of works, lest any man should boast.
>
> **Ephesians 2:5-9**

Faith in Jesus, the Anointed One and His anointing, is the cornerstone message of the New Testament.

> But the *righteousness which is of faith* speaketh on this wise, Say not in thine heart, Who shall ascend into heaven? (that is, to bring Christ down from above:)
>
> Or, Who shall descend into the deep? (that is, to bring up Christ again from the dead.)
>
> *But what saith it? The word is nigh thee, even in thy mouth, and in thy heart: that is, the word of faith, which we preach;*
>
> That if thou shalt confess with thy mouth the Lord Jesus, and shalt believe in thine heart that God hath raised him from the dead, thou shalt be saved.
>
> For with *the heart man believeth* unto righteousness; and with *the mouth confession is made* unto salvation.
>
> For the scripture saith, Whosoever believeth on him shall not be ashamed.
>
> **Romans 10:6-11**

In this passage the words *faith* and *believe* appear several times. In English they are obviously spelled different and appear to have somewhat different meanings. However, in the original Greek the word for *believe* comes directly from the word *faith* (see *Strong's Concordance* #4100 and #4102). The root word for *believe* and *faith* is the same in the Greek, *pist*, which means *faith*. *Faith* is the *noun* form while *believe* is the *verb* form of the word. Although we don't use this word in English, a better translation of the Greek word for *believe* would be *faithing*.

According to Romans, faith works by *believing in your heart* and *confessing with your mouth*. This is how a sinner obtains salvation. This is how a sick person becomes healed. This is how a person in poverty moves into the abundance and blessings of God. Faith is not a formula for getting things, rather it is a *principle* of the Word of God. Jesus Himself stated the importance of *believing in your heart* and *confessing with your mouth* in Mark 11:22–24. If you are not familiar with this passage, you'll want to spend some time studying and meditating on it.

> **And Jesus answering saith unto them, *Have faith in God.***
>
> **For verily I say unto you, That whosoever *shall say* unto this mountain, Be thou removed, and be thou cast into the sea; and shall not doubt in his heart, but shall *believe* that those things which he saith shall come to pass; he shall have whatsoever he saith.**
>
> **Therefore I say unto you, *What things soever ye desire, when ye pray, believe that ye receive them, and ye shall have them.***
>
> **Mark 11:22-24**

Notice how the words *faith* and *believe* are repeated in the same fashion as in the tenth chapter of Romans. *Having faith in God is what makes the anointing work in your life.*

One night in prayer I asked the Lord to show me how I could walk in a greater measure of His anointing. This is what He spoke to my heart.

To be successful in abounding in the anointing you must:

1. Have *the heart of God to love.*

> **For God so *loved* the world, that he gave his only begotten Son, that whosoever believeth in him should not perish, but have everlasting life.**
>
> **John 3:16**

2. Have *the mind of Christ* (the Anointed One and His anointing).

> **Let this *mind* be in you, which was also in Christ Jesus.**
>
> **Philippians 2:5**

3. Realize that *your body is the temple of the Holy Spirit.*

> **What? know ye not that *your body is the temple of the Holy Ghost* which is in you, which ye have of God, and ye are not your own?**

114

**For ye are bought with a price: therefore glorify
God in your body, and in your spirit, which are God's.**
1 Corinthians 6:19-20

God's anointing is made manifest and abounds when
believers have the love of God in their hearts, think the
thoughts of the Anointed One and His anointing, and
realize that they are a "walking-around tabernacle" of the
Holy Spirit. This is what the anointing is all about.

CHAPTER 10
WHO IS IN CONTROL OF THE WEALTH OF THE WORLD?

This question has intrigued man for centuries. Some think governments control the money of certain countries. Others feel a group of international bankers in Europe control the money supply of the world. And some even claim that the gold reserves of Fort Knox and other countries of the world have been removed by these people and stored in Switzerland awaiting a pre–planned financial collapse of the world's banking system.

While these are all plausible secular theories, let's again turn to God's Word to see who is really in control of the "wealth of the world."

> **And I will shake all nations, and the desire of all nations shall come: and I will fill this house with glory, saith the Lord of hosts.**
>
> *The silver is mine, and the gold is mine,* **saith the Lord of hosts.**
>
> Haggai 2:7-8
>
> **For every beast of the forest is mine, and the cattle upon a thousand hills.**
>
> Psalm 50:10

It doesn't take a rocket scientist to conclude that if you owned all the gold, silver, cattle and other animals in this world, you would be a very wealthy person. However, God owns real estate too.

He was, of course, the first real estate developer of both land and sea.

And God said, Let the waters under the heaven be gathered together unto one place, and let the dry land appear: and it was so.

And God called the dry land Earth; and the gathering together of the waters called he Seas: and God saw that it was good.
                                                    Genesis 1:9-10

It is God (not man) Who owns all the cattle, all the gold, all the silver, all the land, and all the sea. Man is only a steward of these possessions. If man is a good steward then he will be steward over more possessions.

His lord said unto him, Well done, thou good and faithful servant: *thou hast been faithful over a few things, I will make thee ruler over many things*: enter thou into the joy of thy lord.
                                                    Matthew 25:21

Man's only power comes from the power that God gives him.

Then saith Pilate unto him, Speakest thou not unto me? knowest thou not that I have power to crucify thee, and have power to release thee?

Jesus answered, *Thou couldest have no power at all against me, except it were given thee from above*.
                                                    John 19:10-11

It is very clear that God has all power (omnipotent power) over man. Man's power, authority, and wealth come from God. However, the fact that God gives each man a free will to make individual choices, confuses many people as to who is the one in control of that power.

Beware that thou forget not the Lord thy God, in not keeping his commandments, and his judgments, and his statutes, which I command thee this day:

Lest when thou hast eaten and art full, and hast built goodly houses, and dwelt therein;

And when thy herds and thy flocks multiply, and thy silver and thy gold is multiplied, and all that thou hast is multiplied;

Then thine heart be lifted up, and thou forget the Lord thy God, which brought thee forth out of the land of Egypt, from the house of bondage;

Who led thee through that great and terrible wilderness, wherein were fiery serpents, and scorpions, and drought, where there was no water; who brought thee forth water out of the rock of flint;

Who fed thee in the wilderness with manna, which thy fathers knew not, that he might humble thee, and that he might prove thee, to do thee good at thy latter end;

And thou say in thine heart, My power and the might of mine hand hath gotten me this wealth.

But thou shalt remember the Lord thy God: for it is he that giveth thee power to get wealth, that he may establish his covenant which he sware unto thy fathers, as it is this day.

And it shall be, if thou do at all forget the Lord thy God, and walk after other gods, and serve them, and worship them, I testify against you this day that ye shall surely perish.

As the nations which the Lord destroyeth before your face, so shall ye perish; because ye would not be obedient unto the voice of the Lord your God.

Deuteronomy 8:11-20

All wealth comes from God. It is God Who gives man the power to get wealth. But what about those people who are prospering that are not "right with God"? You may be shocked by the following scriptures. Nevertheless, they are found in God's Word.

A good man leaveth an inheritance to his children's children: *and the wealth of the sinner is laid up for the just.*

Proverbs 13:22

He that by usury and unjust gain increaseth his substance, *he shall gather it for him that will pity the poor.*

Proverbs 28:8

119

For God giveth to a man that is good in his sight wisdom, and knowledge, and joy: but to the sinner he giveth travail, to gather and to heap up, that he may give to him that is good before God.

Ecclesiastes 2:26

A man to whom God hath given riches, wealth, and honour, so that he wanteth nothing for his soul of all that he desireth, *yet God giveth him not power to eat thereof, but a stranger eateth it:* this is vanity, and it is an evil disease.

Ecclesiastes 6:2

Though he heap up silver as the dust, and prepare raiment as the clay;

He may prepare it, but the just shall put it on, and the innocent shall divide the silver.

Job 27:16-17

But ye shall be named the Priests of the Lord: men shall call you the Ministers of our God: *ye shall eat the riches of the Gentiles,* and in their glory shall ye boast yourselves.

Isaiah 61:6

The scriptures you just read are the key to understanding the "Economics of the Kingdom of God." So next time you become worried because of the prosperity of someone else, realize that either God is blessing them because of their obedience to His Word, or He is simply giving them the task of storing up wealth to be transferred to a "just" person at a later date. Either way, don't worry!

For I was envious at the foolish, when I saw the prosperity of the wicked.

For there are no bands in their death: but their strength is firm.

They are not in trouble as other men; neither are they plagued like other men.

Therefore pride compasseth them about as a chain; violence covereth them as a garment.

> Their eyes stand out with fatness: they have more than heart could wish.
>
> They are corrupt, and speak wickedly concerning oppression: they speak loftily.
>
> They set their mouth against the heavens, and their tongue walketh through the earth.
>
> Therefore his people return hither: and waters of a full cup are wrung out to them.
>
> And they say, How doth God know? and is there knowledge in the most High?
>
> Behold, these are the ungodly, who prosper in the world; they increase in riches.
>
> Verily I have cleansed my heart in vain, and washed my hands in innocence.
>
> For all the day long have I been plagued, and chastened every morning.
>
> If I say, I will speak thus; behold, I should offend against the generation of thy children.
>
> When I thought to know this, it was too painful for me;
>
> Until I went into the sanctuary of God; then understood I their end.
>
> **Psalm 73:3-17**

When you spend time in the "sanctuary" or Word of God, you will begin to see that "the wealth of sinners" will meet an untimely end, for they trust in their riches instead of God. But for now, they do serve a purpose as Solomon states in Ecclesiastes.

> For God giveth to a man that is good in his sight wisdom, and knowledge, and joy: but to the sinner he giveth travail, to gather and to heap up, that he may give to him that is good before God.
>
> **Ecclesiastes 2:26**

> God gives a man wealth, possessions and honor, so that he lacks nothing his heart desires, *but God does not enable him to enjoy them, and a stranger enjoys them instead.*
>
> **Ecclesiastes 6:2 (NIV)**

If that seems strange, you may be surprised to learn that God has transferred wealth from ungodly people to His children before.

Now the children of Israel had done according to the word of Moses, and they had asked from the Egyptians articles of silver, articles of gold, and clothing.

And the Lord had given the people favor in the sight of the Egyptians, so that they granted them what they requested. *Thus they plundered the Egyptians.*
Exodus 12:35-36 (NKJV)

Wealth transfer from the wicked to the righteous is an Economic Law backed by God. You are living in the generation that will see it happen again. However, if you already have riches or if they're in the process of being transferred to you, don't ever trust in them. Not now, not ever.

Charge them that are rich in this world, that they be not highminded, nor trust in uncertain riches, but in the living God, who giveth us richly all things to enjoy.
1 Timothy 6:17

Labour not to be rich: cease from thine own wisdom.

Wilt thou set thine eyes upon that which is not? for riches certainly make themselves wings; they fly away as an eagle toward heaven.
Proverbs 23:4-5

A good man leaveth an inheritance to his children's children: *and the wealth of the sinner is laid up for the just.*
Proverbs 13:22

Here is the fate God allots to the wicked, the heritage a ruthless man receives from the Almighty:

However many his children, their fate is the sword; his offspring will never have enough to eat.

The plague will bury those who survive him, and their widows will not weep for them.

Though he heaps up silver like dust and clothes like piles of clay,

What he lays up the righteous will wear, and the innocent will divide his silver.

The house he builds is like a moth's cocoon, like a hut made by a watchman.

He lies down wealthy, but will do so no more; when he opens his eyes, all is gone.

Terrors overtake him like a flood; a tempest snatches him away in the night.

The east wind carries him off, and he is gone; it sweeps him out of his place.

It hurls itself against him without mercy as he flees headlong from its power.

It claps its hands in derision and hisses him out of his place.
Job 27:13-23 (NIV)

The look on their faces testifies against them; they parade their sin like Sodom; they do not hide it. Woe to them! They have brought disaster upon themselves.

Tell the righteous it will be well with them, for they will enjoy the fruit of their deeds.

Woe to the wicked! Disaster is upon them! They will be paid back for what their hands have done.
Isaiah 3:9-11 (NIV)

Isn't it good to know that God is an equal opportunity employer? He even lets the sinner have the task of storing up wealth so that it can eventually be given to the one who is good before God. And in the final analysis, both the wicked and the righteous will appear before the Throne of God on bended knees.

Let this mind be in you, which was also in Christ Jesus:

Who, being in the form of God, thought it not robbery to be equal with God:

But made himself of no reputation, and took upon him the form of a servant, and was made in the likeness of men:

And being found in fashion as a man, he humbled himself, and became obedient unto death, even the death of the cross.

Wherefore God also hath highly exalted him, and given him a name which is above every name:

That at the name of Jesus every knee should bow, of things in heaven, and things in earth, and things under the earth;

And that every tongue should confess that Jesus Christ is Lord, to the glory of God the Father.

Philippians 2:5-11

This scene can be found in the book of Revelation. It is commonly referred to as "The Great White Throne Judgment." Revelation is probably the most fascinating book of the Bible. It is interesting to note that Revelation is the only book of the Bible that begins by promising a blessing to those who read and take it to heart.

The Revelation of Jesus Christ, which God gave unto him, to shew unto his servants things which must shortly come to pass; and he sent and signified it by his angel unto his servant John:

Who bare record of the word of God, and of the testimony of Jesus Christ, and of all things that he saw.

Blessed is he that readeth, and they that hear the words of this prophecy, and keep those things which are written therein: for the time is at hand.

Revelation 1:1-3

In the book of the Revelation you will also find the Rapture of the church, the four horsemen of the Apocalypse, the 120,000 Jewish evangelists, the seven-year Tribulation, (also known as the "time of Jacob's trouble") worldwide nuclear war, famine, meteors falling from heaven, the antichrist, the false prophet, the mark of the beast, the two witnesses, the prediction of satellite television, the Battle of Armageddon, the return of Jesus Christ with His saints, the judgment of nations, the 1,000-year reign of Christ and the saints, and planet heaven (the New Jerusalem) descending from heaven.

You will want to read the book of Revelation again and again.

The many scriptures of this chapter point out that the wealth of the wicked is laid up for the righteous. As the wicked continue in their unrelenting quest for wealth (leading to their eternal damnation), it is prudent that we remember this scripture from the gospel of Mark.

> **For what shall it profit a man, if he shall gain the whole world, and lose his own soul?**
>
> **Mark 8:36**

This verse should be an important reminder to everyone who seeks wealth, prosperity, and success contrary to God's Word.

God prophesied through David about the kings of the earth who would seek to control the world and set up their own kingdom without God and His Messiah. This is the objective of the New World Order. Notice what God says about this in the second Psalm.

> **Why do the heathen rage, and the people imagine a vain thing?**
>
> *The kings of the earth set themselves, and the rulers take counsel together, against the Lord, and against his anointed, saying,*
>
> **Let us break their bands asunder, and cast away their cords from us.**
>
> **He that sitteth in the heavens shall laugh: the Lord shall have them in derision.**
>
> **Then shall he speak unto them in his wrath, and vex them in his sore displeasure.**

Yet have I set my king upon my holy hill of Zion.

I will declare the decree: the Lord hath said unto me, Thou art my Son; this day have I begotten thee.

Ask of me, and I shall give thee the heathen for thine inheritance, and the uttermost parts of the earth for thy possession.

Thou shalt break them with a rod of iron; thou shalt dash them in pieces like a potter's vessel.

Be wise now therefore, O ye kings: be instructed, ye judges of the earth.

Serve the Lord with fear, and rejoice with trembling.

Kiss the Son, lest he be angry, and ye perish from the way, when his wrath is kindled but a little. Blessed are all they that put their trust in him.

Psalm 2:1-12

God states in His Word that He sits in heaven and laughs at the kings of the earth and man's vain thoughts to fight against Him and His Son. The final fulfillment of this prophecy will be at the Battle of Armageddon which occurs at the end of the Tribulation.

And I saw heaven opened, and behold a white horse; and he that sat upon him was called Faithful and True, and in righteousness he doth judge and make war.

His eyes were as a flame of fire, and on his head were many crowns; and he had a name written, that no man knew, but he himself.

And he was clothed with a vesture dipped in blood: and his name is called The Word of God.

And the armies which were in heaven followed him upon white horses, clothed in fine linen, white and clean.

And out of his mouth goeth a sharp sword, that with it he should smite the nations: and he shall rule them with a rod of iron: and he treadeth the winepress of the fierceness and wrath of Almighty God.

And he hath on his vesture and on his thigh a name written, KING OF KINGS, AND LORD OF LORDS.

126

And I saw an angel standing in the sun; and he cried with a loud voice, saying to all the fowls that fly in the midst of heaven, Come and gather yourselves together unto the supper of the great God;

That ye may eat the flesh of kings, and the flesh of captains, and the flesh of mighty men, and the flesh of horses, and of them that sit on them, and the flesh of all men, both free and bond, both small and great.

And I saw the beast, and the kings of the earth, and their armies, gathered together to make war against him that sat on the horse, and against his army.

And the beast was taken, and with him the false prophet that wrought miracles before him, with which he deceived them that had received the mark of the beast, and them that worshipped his image. These both were cast alive into a lake of fire burning with brimstone.

And the remnant were slain with the sword of him that sat upon the horse, which sword proceeded out of his mouth: and all the fowls were filled with their flesh.

Revelation 19:11-21

We can also find the Battle of Armageddon in the Old Testament.

The burden of the word of the Lord for Israel, saith the Lord, which stretcheth forth the heavens, and layeth the foundation of the earth, and formeth the spirit of man within him.

Behold, I will make Jerusalem a cup of trembling unto all the people round about, when they shall be in the siege both against Judah and against Jerusalem.

And in that day will I make Jerusalem a burdensome stone for all people: all that burden themselves with it shall be cut in pieces, though all the people of the earth be gathered together against it.

In that day, saith the Lord, I will smite every horse with astonishment, and his rider with madness: and I will open mine eyes upon the house of Judah, and will smite every horse of the people with blindness.

And the governors of Judah shall say in their heart, The inhabitants of Jerusalem shall be my strength in the Lord of hosts their God.

In that day will I make the governors of Judah like an hearth of fire among the wood, and like a torch of fire in a sheaf; and they shall devour all the people round about, on the right hand and on the left: and Jerusalem shall be inhabited again in her own place, even in Jerusalem.

The Lord also shall save the tents of Judah first, that the glory of the house of David and the glory of the inhabitants of Jerusalem do not magnify themselves against Judah.

In that day shall the Lord defend the inhabitants of Jerusalem; and he that is feeble among them at that day shall be as David; and the house of David shall be as God, as the angel of the Lord before them.

And it shall come to pass in that day, that I will seek to destroy all the nations that come against Jerusalem.

And I will pour upon the house of David, and upon the inhabitants of Jerusalem, the spirit of grace and of supplications: and they shall look upon me whom they have pierced, and they shall mourn for him, as one mourneth for his only son, and shall be in bitterness for him, as one that is in bitterness for his firstborn.

In that day shall there be a great mourning in Jerusalem, as the mourning of *Hadadrimmon in the valley of Megiddon* ("Valley of Armageddon").

Zechariah 12:1-11

Tip #10

Bible eschatology (the study of the "end times") is one of the most fascinating subjects one could ever study. Dr. J. R. Church and Dr. Jack Van Impe both have a monthly prophetic newsletter as well as many books, video and audio tapes on Bible prophecy and world history. Get in touch with these ministries to increase your understanding of Bible prophecy.

Don't be concerned about the wealth of the world and those who are prospering who aren't serving God. The house of the just *will* be blessed.

> Envy thou not the oppressor, and choose none of his ways.
>
> For the froward is abomination to the Lord: but his secret is with the righteous.
>
> *The curse of the Lord is in the house of the wicked: but he blesseth the habitation of the just.*
>
> Surely he scorneth the scorners: but he giveth grace unto the lowly.
>
> *The wise shall inherit glory: but shame shall be the promotion of fools.*
>
> **Proverbs 3:31-35**

The 37th Psalm also contributes to this theme.

> Fret not thyself because of evildoers, neither be thou envious against the workers of iniquity.
>
> For they shall soon be cut down like the grass, and wither as the green herb.
>
> Trust in the Lord, and do good; so shalt thou dwell in the land, and verily thou shalt be fed.
>
> Delight thyself also in the Lord; and he shall give thee the desires of thine heart.
>
> Commit thy way unto the Lord; trust also in him; and he shall bring it to pass.
>
> And he shall bring forth thy righteousness as the light, and thy judgment as the noonday.
>
> Rest in the Lord, and wait patiently for him: fret not thyself because of him who prospereth in his way, because of the man who bringeth wicked devices to pass.
>
> Cease from anger, and forsake wrath: fret not thyself in any wise to do evil.
>
> For evildoers shall be cut off: but those that wait upon the Lord, they shall inherit the earth.
>
> **Psalm 37:1-9**

The purpose of this wealth transfer is so that the just can be a blessing for the kingdom of God. This is the covenant God made with Abraham.

> **Now the Lord had said unto Abram, Get thee out of thy country, and from thy kindred, and from thy father's house, unto a land that I will shew thee:**
>
> *And I will make of thee a great nation, and I will bless thee, and make thy name great; and thou shalt be a blessing:*
>
> **And I will bless them that bless thee, and curse him that curseth thee: and in thee shall all families of the earth be blessed.**
>
> **Genesis 12:1-3**

This covenant was made before the law of Moses. It was never abolished and is still a part of the covenant of the body of Christ.

> **Christ hath redeemed us from the curse of the law, being made a curse for us: for it is written, Cursed is every one that hangeth on a tree:**
>
> *That the blessing of Abraham might come on the Gentiles through Jesus Christ;* **that we might receive the promise of the Spirit through faith.**
>
> **Galatians 3:13-14**

The purpose of your prosperity and success is so that you can be a blessing to others. Don't ever think for a minute that God wants you to be poor. If you are poor and can't even meet your own family's needs, how will you ever be able to help others? The most selfish thing you ever ask for is just enough to get by. The Word of God even goes as far to say that Jesus became poor that we could be made rich.

> **For ye know the grace of our Lord Jesus Christ, that, though he was rich,** *yet for your sakes he became poor, that ye through his poverty might be rich.*
>
> **2 Corinthians 8:9**

This scripture is hard for some to accept, thus the traditional interpretation means *spiritually* rich. However, it should be taken literally, which is indicated by looking up the word *rich* in *Strong's Concordance*. *4147 plouteo (ploo-teh'-o); from 4148; to be (or become) wealthy (literally or figuratively): KJV— be increased with goods, (be made, wax) rich.*

Contrary to the doctrines of many denominations, God has never expected His children to take a vow of poverty. Rather, He wants you to be in His Word so He can really show you His divine plan for your life. Quit listening to the empty words of man. *Rather, listen to the words of Almighty God, for it is He Who gives you power to get wealth so that you may be a blessing to the people around you.*

God gave Adam dominion and authority over this earth. He then commanded him to be *fruitful, multiply, and replenish.*

> **And God said, Let us make man in our image, after our likeness:** *and let them have dominion* **over the fish of the sea, and over the fowl of the air, and over the cattle, and over all the earth, and over every creeping thing that creepeth upon the earth.**
>
> **So God created man in his own image, in the image of God created he him; male and female created he them.**
>
> *And God blessed them, and God said unto them, Be fruitful, and multiply, and replenish the earth, and subdue it:* **and have dominion over the fish of the sea, and over the fowl of the air, and over every living thing that moveth upon the earth.**
>
> **Genesis 1:26-28**

Adam failed to take dominion over the serpent. However, the first prophecy that Jesus would crush Satan's power appears just a few chapters later in Genesis.

> *And the Lord God said unto the serpent,* **Because thou hast done this, thou art cursed above all cattle, and**

above every beast of the field; upon thy belly shalt thou go, and dust shalt thou eat all the days of thy life:

And I will put enmity between thee and the woman, and between thy seed and her seed; it shall bruise thy head, and thou shalt bruise his heel.

Genesis 3:14-15

The above scripture predicts several things. First of all, this passage prophesies the virgin birth of Jesus. The Bible never refers to the "seed of a woman" except in this passage. It is man's seed that produces offspring. However, Jesus was conceived by the Holy Spirit through the "seed of Mary," thus it was by her seed that Satan's head was to be bruised by the death, burial and resurrection of Jesus. Verse 15 finishes by stating that the serpent would bruise His heel.

Those who were crucified in Roman days would usually die of asphyxiation. The only way they could breathe was to dig their heels into the bottom of the cross and push themselves up and gasp for air. But the pain was so great they could not hold this position for very long. Thus, repeating this process of getting air would leave tremendous bruises on the heels of those who were crucified. In the 22nd Psalm David also prophesies the crucifixion of Jesus Christ, hundreds of years before this form of punishment was ever invented.

My God, my God, why hast thou forsaken me? **why art thou so far from helping me, and from the words of my roaring?**

O my God, I cry in the daytime, but thou hearest not; and in the night season, and am not silent.

But thou art holy, O thou that inhabitest the praises of Israel.

Our fathers trusted in thee: they trusted, and thou didst deliver them.

They cried unto thee, and were delivered: they trusted in thee, and were not confounded.

But I am a worm, and no man; a reproach of men, and despised of the people.

All they that see me laugh me to scorn: they shoot out the lip, they shake the head, saying,

He trusted on the Lord that he would deliver him: let him deliver him, seeing he delighted in him.

But thou art he that took me out of the womb: thou didst make me hope when I was upon my mother's breasts.

I was cast upon thee from the womb: *thou art my God from my mother's belly.*

Be not far from me; for trouble is near; for there is none to help.

Many bulls have compassed me: strong bulls of Bashan have beset me round.

They gaped upon me with their mouths, as a ravening and a roaring lion.

I am poured out like water, and all my bones are out of joint: my heart is like wax; it is melted in the midst of my bowels.

My strength is dried up like a potsherd; and my tongue cleaveth to my jaws; and thou hast brought me into the dust of death.

For dogs have compassed me: the assembly of the wicked have inclosed me: they pierced my hands and my feet.

I may tell all my bones: they look and stare upon me.

They part my garments among them, and cast lots upon my vesture.

But be not thou far from me, O Lord: O my strength, haste thee to help me.

Deliver my soul from the sword; my darling from the power of the dog.

Save me from the lion's mouth: for thou hast heard me from the horns of the unicorns.

I will declare thy name unto my brethren: in the midst of the congregation will I praise thee.

Ye that fear the Lord, praise him; all ye the seed of Jacob, glorify him; and fear him, all ye the seed of Israel.

For he hath not despised nor abhorred the affliction of the afflicted; neither hath he hid his face from him; but when he cried unto him, he heard.

My praise shall be of thee in the great congregation: I will pay my vows before them that fear him.

The meek shall eat and be satisfied: they shall praise the Lord that seek him: your heart shall live for ever.

All the ends of the world shall remember and turn unto the Lord: and all the kindreds of the nations shall worship before thee.

For the kingdom is the Lord's: and he is the governor among the nations.

All they that be fat upon earth shall eat and worship: all they that go down to the dust shall bow before him: and none can keep alive his own soul.

A seed shall serve him; it shall be accounted to the Lord for a generation.

They shall come, and shall declare his righteousness unto a people that shall be born, *that he hath done this.*

Psalm 22:1-31

The ending of verse 31 literally means, "It is finished." Read through the crucifixion accounts in all the gospels. You will be astounded to see that David prophesied this 1,000 years before it happened. After His triumph at the cross, Jesus tells His followers that He now has all authority and power and was giving it to them.

And Jesus came and spake unto them, saying, All power is given unto me in heaven and in earth.

Go ye therefore, and teach all nations, baptizing them in the name of the Father, and of the Son, and of the Holy Ghost:

Teaching them to observe all things whatsoever I have commanded you: and, lo, I am with you alway, even unto the end of the world. Amen.

Matthew 28:18-20

And hath put all things under his feet, and gave him to be the head over all things to the church.

Ephesians 1:22

If you think (as I used to) that the church of the Lord Jesus Christ was a scandal-ridden, powerless congregation of weak–minded people, you obviously haven't been to a church that is on fire for God. If you don't know of one, contact this ministry and we will help you find one near you.

CHAPTER 11
CONCLUSION:
INVESTING FOR SUCCESS

You have a Heavenly Father Who wants to bless you with success and prosperity. It all starts with accepting His Son, Jesus Christ, and receiving the power of the Holy Spirit. Then as you *speak the Word, meditate on the Word, and observe and do God's Word* you cannot help but have victory, dominion, health, prosperity and good success as the scriptures below indicate.

> **Now thanks be unto God, *which always causeth us to triumph in Christ,* and maketh manifest the savour of his knowledge by us in every place.**
> **2 Corinthians 2:14**
> **But thanks be to God, which giveth us the victory through our Lord Jesus Christ.**
> **1 Corinthians 15:57**

> ***I am the Lord that healeth thee.***
> **Exodus 15:26**

> **This book of the law shall not depart out of thy mouth; but thou shalt meditate therein day and night, that thou mayest observe to do according to all that is written therein: for then *thou shalt make thy way prosperous*, and then *thou shalt have good success.***
> **Joshua 1:8**
> **Thus saith the Lord, thy Redeemer, the Holy One of Israel; *I am the Lord thy God which teacheth thee to profit, which leadeth thee by the way that thou shouldest go.***
> **Isaiah 48:17**
> **Believe in the Lord your God, and you shall be established; believe His prophets, and you shall prosper.**
> **2 Chronicles 20:20 (NKJV)**

The final topic of this book deals with investing your money. We've already learned according to the Economics of the Kingdom of God that the wealth of the sinner is laid up for the just. This is the "Macro" Economics of the Kingdom, or the "Big Picture." Now it is time to take a look at the "Micro" Economics of the Kingdom which pertains to the individual.

God's Word tells us that if we give into His kingdom, it will be given back to us by other men (wealth transfer). You mean give to get? If your motives are pure (like planting seeds), that's exactly what God's Word says. Each planting season farmers sow seeds, *expecting to receive* a crop at harvest time. Your Bible is an agricultural book. It is time for the church to start viewing it that way.

Let's look at Jesus' words in the gospel of Luke.

Give, and it shall be given unto you; good measure, pressed down, and shaken together, and running over, shall men give into your bosom. For with the same measure that ye mete withal it shall be measured to you again.
Luke 6:38

When one makes a decision to give, he simultaneously makes the decision how much he will receive back from his giving. How's that? Let's look again at the last sentence of Luke 6:38.

For with the same measure that ye mete withal it shall be measured to you again.

In laymen's terms this means if you give in teaspoon-size amounts, you'll receive back teaspoon-size amounts. If you give shovel-size amounts, you'll receive back shovel-size amounts. If you give in dump-truck load amounts, you'll receive back dump-truck load amounts. Don't worry, you can't outgive God.

Paul also makes these comments in the sixth chapter of Galatians.

Be not deceived; God is not mocked: for whatsoever a man soweth, that shall he also reap.

And let us not be weary in well doing: for in due season we shall reap, if we faint not.

As we have therefore opportunity, let us do good unto all men, especially unto them who are of the household of faith.

Galatians 6:7,9,10

The Economic Laws of sowing and reaping originated with God!

Sowing means to plant seed. Your money is seed. When you plant or sow a portion of your money (seed) in good ground (i.e. churches, ministries, charities, etc.), it dies to you since you no longer can use it. *However, God's Word promises you a return that is many times larger than the investment world has ever seen!*

And he spake many things unto them in parables, saying, Behold, a sower went forth to sow;

And when he sowed, some seeds fell by the way side, and the fowls came and devoured them up:

Some fell upon stony places, where they had not much earth: and forthwith they sprung up, because they had no deepness of earth:

And when the sun was up, they were scorched; and because they had no root, they withered away.

And some fell among thorns; and the thorns sprung up, and choked them:

But other fell into good ground, and brought forth fruit, some an hundredfold, some sixtyfold, some thirtyfold.

Matthew 13:3-8

The eighth verse talks about *thirtyfold, sixtyfold, and a hundredfold return* that the seed brought forth. Do you know how much that is? Let's take a look at other rates of return found in the world.

In today's economic climate, commercial banks are paying a little more than 3 percent return on passbook savings. C.D.'s will pay between 5 percent and 8 percent based on length of the deposit. The Standard & Poors 500 (S & P 500) gained over 25percent from 1992 until 1994. The 1994 December Gold Futures contract had a range from a low of $343 to a high of $426 per ounce (a 20 percent range). Any secular investment that would provide a 20 percent return would be considered outstanding. However, this is only 20 percent of a one-fold return (which is peanuts compared to God's promised rates of return). *It may be hard to believe, but a one-old increase is a 100 percent return! Very few investments ever provide a 100 percent return.*

For example: Let's say you decided to invest $1,000 into God's kingdom by giving to your church's summer youth camp. Miraculously, two weeks later your boss calls you into his office and gives you an unexpected $2,000 bonus for your faithful service.

This bonus would be a one-fold return. The first $1,000 is your initial seed money while the other $1,000 is the one-fold return. This one-fold return represents a 100 percent return. Thus, a ten-fold return would be a 1,000 percent return, a thirty-fold return would be 3,000 percent return; sixty-fold return would be a 6,000 percent return, and a hundred-fold return would be a 10,000 percent return.

God's Word promises that if you will sow in good ground, your return will be between 3,000 percent and 10,000 percent. This is so astronomically high compared to other investments *that you will have to use your faith* if you've never experienced these types of returns before.

Sound too good to be true? Those who doubt God's Word may think so, but others who believe God's Word still do not invest in His kingdom despite these promised rates of return. Since people don't know how or when God "will cause men to give into their bosom," many choose not to invest or fail to invest up to their potential.

Please do not worry about how God will accomplish the task of having men give into your bosom. It's not your problem. It's His! And believe me, for Him it is no problem! So don't go around trying to find the people whot are going to give into your bosom. God will see to it that they find you! In the meantime, find people that you can bless and sow into their bosom. As Jerry Savelle says, "Don't go looking for the man with the water pitcher in his hand. Be the man (or woman) with the water pitcher in your hand! If you do this, rest assured, God will fulfill His Word!

> **So shall my word be that goeth forth out of my mouth: it shall not return unto me void, but it shall accomplish that which I please, and it shall prosper in the thing whereto I sent it.**
> **Isaiah 55:11**

Here lies the trade-off between the world's investment vehicles vs. investing in God's kingdom. It is very easy to calculate the rate of return and the maturity date on most investments. Many of the world's investments state in detail how the principal and interest will be repaid to the investor. However, when giving into God's kingdom you must trust Him since you cannot precisely compute the return nor the date that it is coming back to you. Though be assured, it will come in due season, repaid to you between 3,000 percent and 10,000 percent.

Note: If you read the fine print on most investments, the principal is not guaranteed. Only government backed securities and bank accounts up to $100,000 are guaranteed. But even then, they're only as solid as the United States government. How's that for security? Wouldn't you rather have confidence that your investment dollars were backed by God?

Most people have several accounts with different companies. They have bank accounts, checking accounts, brokerage accounts, credit card accounts, department store accounts, etc. However, did you know that God has opened a heavenly account just for those who invest in His kingdom? You've already learned what kind of interest He pays. You should also know He has never defaulted to anyone.

> **Now ye Philippians know also, that in the beginning of the gospel, when I departed from Macedonia, *no church communicated with me as concerning giving and receiving, but ye only.***
>
> **For even in Thessalonica ye sent once and again unto my necessity.**
>
> **Not because I desire a gift: but *I desire fruit that may abound to your account.***
>
> **But I have all, and abound: I am full, having received of Epaphroditus the things which were sent from you, an odour of a sweet smell, a sacrifice acceptable, wellpleasing to God.**
>
> ***But my God shall supply all your need according to his riches in glory by Christ Jesus.***
>
> **Philippians 4:15-19**

The 17th verse concludes with the statement that fruit (return) may abound to your account. This was because of their giving.

Let's look at the same verse in the *New International Version:*

> **Not that I am looking for a gift, but I am looking for what may be *credited to your account.***

Isn't it good to know that God makes *credits* to your account based on your giving to Him. Any good accountant will tell you the more credits you have, the better off your account is going to be.

Oral Roberts once preached on Trinity Broadcasting Network (TBN) expounding on Philippians 4:15b, "No church communicated with me as concerning giving and *receiving,* but ye only." He stated that the word *receiving* in *Strong's Concordance* meant *receipting.* I looked this up and he was right. He went on to say that God gives you receipts and credits your heavenly account when you give. You can then cash in these receipts in much the same way that you withdraw funds from your savings account in times of need.

Believe it or not, you can actually loan God money too. That's right! Instead of trusting your money to someone else, why not make loans to God? With Him you can count on getting your money back!

> **He that hath pity upon the poor lendeth unto the Lord; and that which he hath given will he pay him again.**
>
> **Proverbs 19:17**

You can be assured, God will repay the loans you make to Him. Had the rich young ruler of Mark 10 trusted Him, he would have inherited eternal life *plus received back all his riches!*

> **And when he was gone forth into the way, there came one running, and kneeled to him, and asked him, Good Master, what shall I do that I may inherit eternal life?**
>
> **And Jesus said unto him, Why callest thou me good? there is none good but one, that is, God.**
>
> **Thou knowest the commandments, Do not commit adultery, Do not kill, Do not steal, Do not bear false witness, Defraud not, Honour thy father and mother.**
>
> **And he answered and said unto him, Master, all these have I observed from my youth.**
>
> **Then Jesus beholding him loved him, and said unto him, *One thing thou lackest: go thy way, sell whatsoever thou hast, and give to the poor, and thou***

> shalt have treasure in heaven: and come, take up the cross, and follow me.
>
> And he was sad at that saying, and went away grieved: for he had great possessions.
>
> And Jesus looked round about, and saith unto his disciples, How hardly shall they that have riches enter into the kingdom of God!
>
> **Mark 10:17-23**

This man trusted in his riches rather than in Jesus, the Word of God. The fact that he had great possessions was a testimony that God had blessed him for keeping the law. But obviously he did not fully have faith that God would repay him. (Proverbs 19:17.) Had he followed the instructions of Jesus, he would have had treasure in heaven and also in his present life on earth. How's that? Let's read further in the gospel of Mark.

> And they were astonished out of measure, saying among themselves, Who then can be saved?
>
> And Jesus looking upon them saith, With men it is impossible, but not with God: for with God all things are possible.
>
> Then Peter began to say unto him, Lo, we have left all, and have followed thee.
>
> And Jesus answered and said, Verily I say unto you, There is no man that hath left house, or brethren, or sisters, or father, or mother, or wife, or children, or lands, for my sake, and the gospel's,
>
> *But he shall receive an hundredfold now in this time,* houses, and brethren, and sisters, and mothers, and children, and lands, with persecutions; and in the world to come eternal life.
>
> But many that are first shall be last; and the last first.
>
> **Mark 10:26-31**

That just blows the doors off religious tradition that claims that Christians are to take a vow of poverty while on earth. Oh! One other thing. Did you notice how the apostles were astonished when Jesus made the comment how hard it was for the rich to enter the kingdom of God? Why would they be astonished if they were poor men as religious tradition usually teaches? Let's look at their words again.

And they were astonished out of measure, saying among themselves, *Who then can be saved?*

Mark 10:26

They were astonished because they were men of substance and possessions (research the scriptures closely if this is hard for you to believe). Jesus told them it was hard for rich men to enter the kingdom of God. This caused them much concern. However, Jesus replies:

And Jesus looking upon them saith, With men it is impossible, but not with God: *for with God all things are possible.*

Mark 10:27

Unfortunately, most people find God's Word hard to accept and will continue to invest in the temporary (seen) things of this world, reaping very little. Successful people will continue to invest and reap in the eternal (unseen) things, which yield far greater returns.

While we look not at the things which are seen, but at the things which are not seen: *for the things which are seen are temporal; but the things which are not seen are eternal.*

2 Corinthians 4:18

Successful investors who have faith in God's Word will reap thirty-fold (3,000 percent), sixty-fold (6,000 percent), and hundred-fold (10,000 percent) not only in wealth, but in every aspect of their life when they invest in His kingdom. But you might ask, "How long will God continue giving these rates of return (harvest) to those people who sow seed into His kingdom?"

For the answer, turn to the eighth chapter of Genesis.

While the earth remaineth, seedtime and harvest, and cold and heat, and summer and winter, and day and night *shall not cease.*

Genesis 8:22

While the world worries about inflation, deflation, stagflation, recessions, depressions, the stock market, the federal reserve, the European Economic Community, and the decline of the dollar, God promises the law of seedtime and harvest will always be in effect.

Regardless of the economic conditions, *God promises a 3,000 percent, 6,000 percent and 10,000 percent return to those who invest in His kingdom.*

As a commodity trader I have had considerable investment and trading experience over the years. However, I have never had or even seen these types of returns in the commodity markets. Occasionally, there might be an investor who hit it big in the markets but eventually he would lose it all in the end. In the world of investments, if you were ever able to receive a 20 percent return (which is 20 percent of one-fold) on your investment, it would be considered "hitting a home run." *However, I have personally experienced (and I'm still experiencing) returns between 3,000 percent and 10,000 percent when investing (sowing) into the kingdom of God with my finances.*

Isn't it good to know that God also practices what He preaches since He sowed the greatest gift of all when He gave His Son to the world.

For God so loved the world, that *he gave his only begotten Son,* that whosoever believeth in him should not perish, but have everlasting life.

For God sent not his Son into the world to condemn the world; but that the world through him might be saved.

He that believeth on him is not condemned: but he that believeth not is condemned already, because he hath not believed in the name of the only begotten Son of God.

And this is the condemnation, that light is come into the world, and men loved darkness rather than light, because their deeds were evil.

For every one that doeth evil hateth the light, neither cometh to the light, lest his deeds should be reproved.

But he that doeth truth cometh to the light, that his deeds may be made manifest, that they are wrought in God.

John 3:16-21

Most people have never read past the 16th verse. In it lies the explanation why not all people choose to believe in Him. Let's look again at the scriptures immediately following John 3:16.

For God sent not his Son into the world to condemn the world; but that the world through him might be saved.

He that believeth on him is not condemned: but he that believeth not is condemned already, because he hath not believed in the name of the only begotten Son of God.

And this is the condemnation, that light is come into the world, and men loved darkness rather than light, because their deeds were evil.

For every one that doeth evil hateth the light, neither cometh to the light, lest his deeds should be reproved.

But he that doeth truth cometh to the light, that his deeds may be made manifest, that they are wrought in God.

verses 17-21

Everyday, people either choose to walk in the kingdom of darkness or to walk in the Light of God's Word. *Choose this day whom you'll serve. Your success depends on it!*

And if it seem evil unto you to serve the Lord, *choose you this day whom ye will serve;* whether the gods which your fathers served that were on the other side of the flood, or the gods of the Amorites, in whose land ye dwell: but as for me and my house, we will serve the Lord.

Joshua 24:15

Choose to serve God and reap the promise of abounding in all things.

But this I say, He which soweth sparingly shall reap also sparingly; and *he which soweth bountifully shall reap also bountifully.*

Every man according as he purposeth in his heart, so let him give; not grudgingly, or of necessity: for God loveth a cheerful giver.

And God is able to make all grace abound toward you; *that ye, always having all sufficiency in all things, may abound to every good work:*

(As it is written, He hath dispersed abroad; he hath given to the poor: his righteousness remaineth for ever.

Now he that ministereth seed to the sower both minister bread for your food, and multiply your seed sown, and increase the fruits of your righteousness.

2 Corinthians 9:6-10

I refer to this scripture as "The Economics of the Clearinghouse." When you are actively involved in sowing and reaping (investing and profiting), you become like a clearinghouse. In the commodity futures industry, a clearing house matches the trades of buyers with the trades of sellers. Clearinghouses handle millions of dollars each day as money continually changes hands between buyers and sellers.

What is the purpose of the clearinghouse? Its purpose is to facilitate business. What is its reward? It receives commissions on the trading. When you invest in the kingdom of God, you act as a clearinghouse, facilitating trade for the Glory of God as He has commanded. You will then reap commissions (profiting both spiritually and physically) because of your obedience to His Word. God has ordained this Economic Law of seedtime and harvest (which is also called sowing and reaping or investing and profiting) to work in all generations. God is a businessman!

One day you will give an account for all the trading you have conducted for the kingdom of God.

> **And it came to pass, that when he was returned, having received the kingdom, then he commanded these servants to be called unto him, to whom he had given the money, *that he might know how much every man had gained by trading.***
>
> **Luke 19:15**

Most people in the church today have failed to see that Jesus is a businessman. The very first recorded words of Jesus are found in the gospel of Luke.

> **And He said to them, "Why did you seek Me? Did you not know that I must be about My Father's business?"**
>
> **Luke 2:49 (NKJV)**

In fact, His first words are in the form of a question. **Did you not know that I must be about My Father's business?**

No Chief Executive Officer in the history of the world has ever put together an organization such as the church of the Lord Jesus Christ. Unlike most companies, His influence is not limited to any particular nation, country, race, creed, color, socio-economic class, or generation for that matter. He started working for His Father at a young age but didn't take over the company until He was 30 years old. He then personally promoted The Produce of Abundant and Everlasting Life, spending onlythree and one half years "out in the field." The success of His organization is most surprising to modern CEO's. He mentored only twelve men to take over the field work before returning to a management position back at the Home Offce. Before He left, there was even some controversy when one of the twelve, His accountant, betrayed Him, embezzled money, and later committed suicide. However, the most remarkable fact is that He accomplished so much since living about 2,000 years ago, unable to use computers, telephones, faxes, pagers, automobiles, or airplanes to spread His Message to the whole world. Yet, most of these inventions and the increase of knowledge which led to them came from His followers and family members. To this day, you can't drive down the street without seeing one of His branch offices on the corner. And His Book, (He didn't actually write it with His own hands but inspired others to) has sold more copies than all of the other books ever written combined. Surely His teachings, methods, procedures and accomplishments must be noted by today's businessman.

So far in this book, we have only discussed investing in the kingdom of God (offerings). Now let's take a look at tithing. Tithing is the final essential ingredient for the believer's success. If you've never tithed, you've never given any offerings either since you still owe back tithes. As God's Word states in Malachi, if you don't pay your tithes, you are robbing God and are not covered under His health and financial protection plan.

> **Will a man rob God? Yet ye have robbed me. But ye say, Wherein have we robbed thee? In tithes and offerings.**

> **Ye are cursed with a curse: for ye have robbed me, even this whole nation.**

> **Bring ye all the tithes into the storehouse, that there may be meat in mine house, and prove me now herewith, saith the Lord of hosts, if I will not open you the windows of heaven, and pour you out a blessing, that there shall not be room enough to receive it.**

> And I will rebuke the devourer for your sakes, and he shall not destroy the fruits of your ground; neither shall your vine cast her fruit before the time in the field, saith the Lord of hosts.

> And all nations shall call you blessed: for ye shall be a delightsome land, saith the Lord of hosts.

> **Malachi 3:8-12**

Tithing is the topic that makes most people shudder. Why is that? *Because most people do not tithe!* What is the tithe? The tithe means 10 percent, *the first 10 percent of your income, your firstfruits.* As Buddy Harrison says, "People tithed before, during, and after the law, because tithing is a law!"

It is widely estimated that less than 20 percent of the church tithes on a consistent basis. This means that the church is operating on an 80 percent deficiency because only 20 percent of the people are tithing. No wonder many churches are having cash flow problems!

As members of the body of Christ, we are commanded by God to give 10 percent of our gross income to our local church, the storehouse. Malachi states that the purpose of the tithe is that there may be *meat in the house of the Lord to do the work of the ministry.* God then promises four things to the individuals, churches and ministries who are obedient in paying their tithes.

In Malachi, God promises that if we tithe He will:

1. Open the windows of heaven to you.

2. Pour you out a blessing that you cannot contain.

3. Rebuke the devourer for your sakes.

4. Honor you as all nations call you blessed.

In the book of Deuteronomy we also read about the tithe which is called the firstfruits.

> And it shall be, when thou art come in unto the land which the Lord thy God giveth thee for an inheritance, and possessest it, and dwellest therein;

That thou shalt take of the first of all the fruit of the earth, which thou shalt bring of thy land that the Lord thy God giveth thee, and shalt put it in a basket, and shalt go unto the place which the Lord thy God shall choose to place his name there.

And thou shalt go unto the priest that shall be in those days, and say unto him, I profess this day unto the Lord thy God, that I am come unto the country which the Lord sware unto our fathers for to give us.

Deuteronomy 26:1-3

And now, behold, I have brought the firstfruits of the land, which thou, O Lord, hast given me. And thou shalt set it before the Lord thy God, and worship before the Lord thy God.

Deuteronomy 26:10

Honour the Lord with thy substance, and with the firstfruits of all thine increase:

So shall thy barns be filled with plenty, and thy presses shall burst out with new wine.

Proverbs 3:9-10

It is a sad day when ministers won't teach on the subject of tithing, fearing that their people who are already giving might get mad and leave for another church. The Word of God says you are responsible for paying your tithes regardless of what church you attend. Each time you get your paycheck, immediately write out a check for your tithe before you do anything. Do this cheerfully as your High Priest, Jesus, is listening to your profession (confession) when you bring your tithes and offerings to Him.

The giving of your tithes and offerings is one of the highest forms of worship. The tithe is paid to God through the church that you make your home. Offerings can be given to your church, ministries, charities, people, etc. Just be sure to invest in "good ground"! Also make a special effort to support the ministries that are "feeding you the

Word". Avoid giving to ministries that are in constant crisis and are always begging for money. Don't forget to give to the poor but also give to givers. If you have never tithed, simply repent and start doing so immediately! Malachi 3:10 says that God wants you to test Him on this matter and see if He will not open the windows of heaven for a tither.

We have already learned a great deal from Abraham, but did you know that he was also a tither?

> **And Melchizedek king of Salem brought forth bread and wine: and he was the priest of the most high God.**
>
> **And he blessed him, and said, Blessed be Abram of the most high God, possessor of heaven and earth:**
>
> **And blessed be the most high God, which hath delivered thine enemies into thy hand.** *And he gave him tithes of all.*
>
> **Genesis 14:18-20**

Did you notice the first reference in the Bible to the "bread and wine" (communion) was just two verses ahead of Abraham's tithing? Both are extremely important. Likewise, the New Testament also speaks about Abraham paying his tithes.

> **For this Melchisedec, king of Salem, priest of the most high God, who met Abraham returning from the slaughter of the kings, and blessed him;**
>
> *To whom also Abraham gave a tenth part of all;* **first being by interpretation King of righteousness, and after that also King of Salem, which is, King of peace;**
>
> **Without father, without mother, without descent, having neither beginning of days, nor end of life; but made like unto the Son of God; abideth a priest continually.**
>
> **Hebrews 7:1-3**

Abraham tithed to Melchisedec who was "made like unto the Son of God." Therefore, we, "who are of the faith of Abraham," should tithe to our High Priest, Jesus Christ, the Son of God. As was said earlier, we do this by giving 10 percent of our gross income to our local storehouse (church).

In the final analysis, your long-term success (as well as your church's and other ministries), will be determined upon obedience to Malachi 3:8-12. Only then will you truly have good success.

TIP #11

For further study on investing, giving, sowing, reaping, and tithing, contact John Avanzini's ministry. He produces more helpful information on the principles of Biblical Economics than anyone I have ever seen. Since Economics was my major in college, I thought I knew all there was to know about Economics. Was I ever wrong! College failed to teach me that God is "The Founder of Economics" and that His Word contains a wealth of economic information. In John Avanzini's books, tapes, and debt–free ministry, he shows people how they can have financial independence according to God's Word. He also spends much time on the topics of giving, tithing, and sowing and reaping. Those who are truly interested in furthering their financial success will not hesitate to contact his ministry.

FINAL TIP #12

Each time you receive a paycheck, bonus, or any type of income, pay your 10 percent tithe, and then pay yourself 10 percent too! Put this money into a savings account and don't touch it. Let it grow! Don't let anyone talk you into spending this money. If you will begin doing this now, you will be amazed how much you can save in a short period of time. It may seem difficult at first but if you are disciplined, you will be on your way to building a very large nest egg. Continue also to invest in the kingdom of God through offerings.

We've learned from the Economics of the Kingdom that it is God Who gives you the power to get wealth. (Deuteronomy 8:18.) He is the One Who will teach you how to profit. (Isaiah 48:17.) He controls all the wealth of the world and is in the process of transferring it from the sinners to the righteous (Proverbs 13:22) for the purpose of financing the gospel of Jesus Christ for this final end-time harvest.

God has raised up people like Paul and Jan Crouch (and many others) who have been faithful in bringing the message of Jesus to the whole wide world. Paul and Jan are founders of Trinity Broadcasting Network (TBN) which began over 20 years ago. TBN now includes a network of over 500 television stations as well as a shortwave radio network which is proclaiming the gospel of Jesus Christ all around the world. As a teenager, I'm sorry to say I ridiculed what Paul and Jan Crouch were doing. However, 10 years later I became one of their many faithful partners.

It takes millions and millions of dollars to bring the gospel of Jesus Christ to the world through television, radio, print, and other ministries and methods. *This is the real purpose for wealth and the message implied by the title of this book.* Jesus Himself prophesied that the gospel would be preached to the entire world and then the end would come. We are very close to the end of this age. No other generation has witnessed the fulfillment of Bible prophecy like this one. (Matthew 24:32.)

And this gospel of the kingdom shall be preached in all the world for a witness unto all nations; and then shall the end come.

Matthew 24:14

May God richly bless you as you invest in the kingdom of God!

ABOUT THE AUTHOR

Kurtis Ward is President of KIS Futures Trading, Inc., a commodity brokerage firm headquartered in Oklahoma City, Oklahoma. He is also a District Sales Agent with Data Transmission Network, a supplier of electronic market data and weather information systems. Kurtis has written articles for various publications on business topics as well as biblical truths and promises that are found in God's Word.

Kurtis teaches and conducts financial seminars on the subject of "The Economics of the Kingdom of God." He is the President and Founder of Economics of the Kingdom Publishing Company. Kurtis has also spoken to bankers, farmers, and ranchers all across the United States on commodity futures and options.

During the Persian Gulf War of 1990–1991, Kurtis became very interested in Bible prophecy. In the Middle East, Saddam Hussein (an Arab) had invaded another Arab country, yet was bombing Israel with SCUD missiles at the same time. Kurtis became fascinated when he learned that this struggle between the Arabs and Jews began long ago. Genesis, the first book of the Bible, records that Abraham had two sons, Ishmael and Isaac.The Arabs descended from Ishmael while the Jewish people descended from Isaac. The conflict between Jews and Arabs continues today in the Middle East. In Revelation, the last book of the Bible, the events of the "Last Days" take place in the Middle East culminating with the Battle of Armageddon.

It was during this intensive prophetic Bible study that Kurtis finally believed that God did in fact send His Son,

Jesus, the Messiah, to the earth as recorded in the gospels of Matthew, Mark, Luke, and John. Kurtis also received the Holy Spirit as recorded in Acts 19:2–6. The Word of God then became the most important thing in his life.

Kurtis and his wife Regina are members of Church of the Harvest in Oklahoma City, Oklahoma. Regina is active in the music ministry and has appeared on several Christian recordings. Kurtis is a teacher of the Men's Discipleship Groups.

Kurtis and Regina have a daughter, Taylor, and live in Oklahoma City, Oklahoma.

The following is a list of ministries that preach and teach the uncompromised Word of God. They are excellent ministries for investing into the kingdom of God. There are of course others, but I have personally studied and followed these ministries. Their programs, books, and tapes have been valuable instruments in furthering my knowledge of the Word. I highly recommend them to you.

Trinity Broadcasting Network
Paul and Jan Crouch
Box A
Santa Ana, CA 92711-2101

Kenneth Copeland Ministries
Fort Worth, TX 76192

Jerry Savelle Ministries
Box 748
Crowley, TX 76036

Jack Van Impe Ministries
Box 7004
Troy, MI 48007

Mike Murdock
P. O. Box 99
Dallas, TX 75221

700 Club
Christian Broadcasting Network
Pat Robertson
Virginia Beach, VA 23463

Christian Coalition
Box 1990
Chesapeake, VA 23327

This Week in Bible Prophecy
Peter & Paul LaLonde
Box 1440
Niagara Falls, NY 14302-1440

John Avanzini
Box 1057
Hurst, TX 76053

The King Is Coming
Dave Breese
Box 907
Colton, CA 92324-0907

High Praise Ministries
Danny Chambers
Box 23711
Oklahoma City, OK 73123

John Hagee Ministries
Box 1400
San Antonio, TX 78295-1400

Benny Hinn Ministries
Box 90
Orlando, FL 32802-0090

Prophecy In the News
J. R. Church
Box 7000
Oklahoma City, OK 73153-7000

Rod Parsley
World Harvest Church
P. O. Box 32932
Columbus, OH 43232

World Changers Ministries
Creflo A. Dollar, Jr.
P. O. Box 490124
College Park, GA 30349

Fellowship of Christian Farmers, Int.
(FCFI)
Box 15
Lexington, IL 61753

Fred Price
Crenshaw Christian Center
P. O. Box 90000
Los Angeles, CA 90009

Charles Capps Ministries
Box 69
England, AR 72046

Promise Keepers
Box 1442
Arvada, CO 80001-1442

Larry Burkett
Christian Financial Concepts
Box 2377
Gainesville, GA 30503-2377

Kenneth Hagin Ministries
Broken Arrow, OK 74012

Oral Roberts Ministries
7777 S. Lewis
Tulsa, OK 74171

If this book was given to you and has been a blessing to you, contact Kurtis Ward by phone or mail.

To order multiple books for large groups, salespersons, businessmen groups, schools, or to book a speaking engagement please call:

1–800–256–2555

or write:

Economics of the Kingdom
Kurtis Ward
3232 W. Britton Road
Suite 170
Oklahoma City, OK 73120